DOMINANCE AND LANGUAGE

A New Perspective on Sexism

Roberta W. Caldie

UNIVERSITY
PRESS OF
AMERICA

Copyright © 1981 by
Roberta W. Caldie

University Press of America,Inc.™

P.O. Box 19101, Washington, D.C. 20036

Printed in the United States of America

ISBN: 0-8191-1967-9(Perfect)
0-8191-1966-0(Case)

Library of Congress Number: 81-40141

DEDICATION

This book is dedicated to my family,
where caring dominates and language is
recognized as one of many ways to express
those experiences people share.

ACKNOWLEDGEMENTS

There are many individuals without whose help this book could not have been completed. All of the teachers in my life made powerful contributions. My friends who cared for my children while I worked, my students who stimulated me and supported my progress, and my colleagues at Bethune-Cookman College, helped more than they realize.

To Aileen St. Leger, my warmest thanks for much more than an excellent typing job. Her friendly encouragement, high standards and constant readiness to work were an inspiration.

To the members of the Women's Movement, I owe much gratitude for showing me that a woman's place is everywhere.

Finally, to my children who grew up with me, who share every adventure with a willingness to grow and to try, and who take pride in my efforts, I give most loving thanks.

TABLE OF CONTENTS

viii

LIST OF FIGURES

LIST OF TABLES

LIST OF APPENDICES

Chapter 1:   INTRODUCTION

DOMINANCE AND LANGUAGE: A New Perspective on Sexism

THE PROBLEM:

The American English language has repeatedly
been criticized for being sexist and contributing
to the lower self-esteem and achievement levels of
females throughout our society (Gornick 1971,
Lipman-Blumen and Tickamyer 1971, Cantrell 1974).
The charges of sexism in our language rest upon
assumptions that language is a powerful socializing
agent, and that as such, it can mold the self-con-
cept, achievement motivation and sex-role stereotypes of all the users of this language. Therefore,
thoughtful scrutiny has been directed at the male-
dominant pronoun selection, word order and figures
of speech we use in our everyday conversation, as
well as in official documents, tests and literature.[1]

Defenders of the contemporary American English
language assert that language merely reflects a
culture, and that concerns over sexism should be
directed toward popular attitudes and beliefs, and
not toward linguistic characteristics of communications (Williams 1971). Academicians set the stage
for this current issue in the early 1940's when the
fields of sociolinguistics and psycholinguistics
sprang up around the Sapir-Whorfian hypothesis of
linguistic relativism.[2] These fields have ever
since been dealing with the intriguing relationships between thought and language and culture.

Before the recent examination of sexism in our
language, analogous charges and investigations were
made concerning racism, nationalism, professional-
ism (jargon) and regionalism. Liza Doolittle (of
Pygmalian fame) has come to stand for the position
that language determines the person, while the
reverse position is illustrated by the drug cult,
a group with shared experience giving rise to an
entire dialect.[3]

Whether human experience shapes language or language shapes human experience, social science and social policy have in the last twenty years been quite sensitive to the relationship between language, socioeconomic status and mobility. Drawing parallels between established studies of racism and current studies of sexism, a basic question has been: Was the existence of "white English" and "black English" a causal factor impeding race relations, or were the racial groups so separate (due to non-linguistic factors) as to require different language habits? In other words, does language promote differences, reflect them, or both? The same question was asked of other ethnic, regional and interest groups, always with no conclusive answer, and this study now asks it of male pronoun dominance in relation to sexism in our culture.

The purpose of this analytical study is to discover if there is a relationship between the degree of male-pronoun dominance in the American English language and the relative status of males and females referred to by that language. Pursuit of this question can yield information having both practical and theoretical significance. On the practical side, the effectiveness of non-sexist language which has been demanded by women's rights advocates can be assessed. On the theoretical side, this research question explores the relationship between cultural attitudes and language. There is a need for empirical data to assess the interrelationships between male pronoun dominance and sex role conceptualizations and covert predispositions toward discrimination. Such biases may be based on conditioned associations between masculine terms and positive human qualities and activities, leaving female terms unattached to positive concepts and instead, conceptualized by antithesis, or simply never well conceptualized at all (McClelland 1965, Bardwick 1971).

A case illustration where masculinity and positive attributes are fused is found in this well known selection written in 1958 by David McClelland,

2

referring to the personality characteristic of
achievement motivation:

> "The person who is achievement moti-
> vated takes pride in his work when he is
> held responsible for his actions, when he
> is informed of his level of performance
> and there are criteria of performance, and
> when there is an element or risk involved
> (when he is not certain of success)."

Would the reader of this passage respond in
any significant way to the exclusive reference to
males? If the language were simplified but still
masculinized, and offered to preschool children,
would it convince little girls that achievement
motivation is not relevant to them? Even more
importantly, what "mind set" effect would such
traditional language perpetuate in the actual target group of professional psychologists, socio-
logists and educators who read McClelland's arti-
cles? That the exclusive reference to males may
have some bearing on the common finding that males
excel in achievement situations is a possibility
worth exploring.

True to the concrete _form_ of McClelland's passage, males score far higher than females on indices
of achievement motivation when in competitive situations (Horner 1971, Monohan 1974, Martin 1973).
Maccoby (1974) suggests that males' higher achievements in their professions may be due to sex differences in initiative, differences which may reflect
conditioned associations between masculinity and
positive characteristics. Simplistic excuses[4] for
the exclusive use of the male pronoun in the quoted
selection usually revolve around "he" expediently
signifying all people, yet that "he" in the achievement motivation description has a prophetic quality.
"The language has worked with remarkable success in
making it possible for man to perpetuate himself as
master, to foster the illusion that women are dependent, and in fact, to subjugate women" (Cantrell
1974, p. 32). Male dominance in language may not
only reflect but also be involved in the perpetua-

tion of cultural male dominance. Again, the question is whether language causes or reflects attitudes and values. To test the connection between male pronoun dominance and sexism, criteria must be established for discriminatory language style.[5]

The crucial questions are: Is Cantrell correct about the sexist intent of male pronoun dominance, and if so, how can language subjugate women? In the abundance of current feminist literature, there appear testimonial after testimonial to the prejudicial effect and intent of standard American English. Even David Guralnik, editor-in-chief of Webster's New Worl Dictionary of the American Language stated in a prepublication interview[6] that our language is "perhaps the most masculine of all the languages of Europe" since there is no neuter singular personal pronoun, and that the purpose of the extensive masculinization of English was to "indoctrinate the woman from early childhood into not moving our of her assigned sphere." Therefore, language seems both to reflect and to perpetuate a male-dominated society.

However, in that same interview, Guralnik addressed the issue of linguistic change by declaring that "language serves a purpose, and words survive while they are useful." Since language can be considered the "litmus paper of culture," as rules change so should the language change, in parallel. Thus, there appears to be a recurring paradox, that language is structured to indoctrinate and to preserve the status quo, yet language is living and responsive to changing social conditions. The theory of Guralnik, a foremost lexicographer, has plunged theoretical researchers into deeper confusion over the relationship between thought and language and culture.

ORGANIZATION OF THIS STUDY

To examine and to isolate critical questions, and to make an inroad into the confusion, Chapter 2 will be a literature review organized around three research questions. Each question has associated

4

with it empirical hypotheses based on general theoretical issues and considerations from the literature. The questions are:

1. Does the degree of male pronoun dominance in our language have any effect
   on the way people bestow status upon
   males and females?

   A. EMPIRICAL HYPOTHESES

      1. Standard (male pronoun domi-
         nant) English will be associ-
         ated with a pro-male bias, all
         other things being equal.

      2. Non-sexist (he/she, she/he,
         neutral pronouns) English will
         be associated with pro-female
         bias, all other things being
         equal.

      3. Itemized (no pronouns, control
         condition) English will not be
         associated with any sex bias.

   B. THEORETICAL ISSUE: Do the form and
      content of language develop and main-
      tain sex roles and biases?

2. Do attitudes, in this case the degree of
   role rigidity, which a person displays
   have any effect on the way this person
   bestows status upon males and females?

   A. EMPIRICAL HYPOTHESES

      1. The greater the role rigidity
         score of the subject (an organis-
         mic variable measured by the Role
         Rigidity Scale) the stronger the
         pro-male bias (or the greater the
         discrimination against females).

5

2. Other demographic variables of the subject will moderate the effect of the experimental treatment (language style) on the criterion (sex bias) operating through the intervening variable of role conceptualization.

3. Subjects drawn from a population of National Organization for Women (N.O.W.) affiliates would display significant pro-female biases across all treatment conditions.

B. THEORECTICAL ISSUE: Do our role conceptualizations influence or override the effects of language styles in communication?

3. What effect would the condition of non-sexist English have on the way people bestow status upon males and females?

A. EMPIRICAL HYPOTHESES

1. Subjects drawn from a population of Kiwanis Club members will show a backlash effect (augmented pro-male bias, or increased anti-female bias) under the non-sexist language treatment condition.[7]

2. There will be a positive correlation between age of subject and tendency to backlash (as described above).

B. THEORETICAL ISSUE: How do written and spoken language change, both officially and unofficially, and what happens when social policy imposes "unnatural" language change upon people (e.g., legislation requiring non-sexist language in federal publications)?[8]

The first two research questions attempt to
discover the relative strengths of the forces which
Sapir and Whorf were evaluating, however, this study
restricts the domain of culture to the phenomenon
of sex bias. The first question explores language
as a cause of bias, and the second question consi-
ders whether preexisting biases influence how one
receives, processes and generates language. Since
this empirical study deals exclusively with college-
aged and older subjects, a severe limitation of
this second question is that it cannot assess the
degree to which language was a potent socializing
force in the origins of the biases reflected in the
Role Rigidity Scale. Rigidity is presented as a
fait accompli, which is of much practical significance but sheds little theoretical light.

Finally, the third question is entirely aimed
at applications of the findings from the first question's hypotheses. Official guidelines issued by
private industry, institutions and government
agencies at this time increasingly impose non-
sexist language on all writers for their publications. Before such drastic impositions are laid
down, mechanisms of natural language change along
with artificial attempts to impose change should
be evaluated. The literature describes such mechanisms and actual attempts only in the broadest terms,
leaving much to be learned from the experimental
results of this study.

Following Chapter 2, the review of relevant
literature, the experimental design will be set
forth in Chapter 3. Briefly previewing, the independent variable is the degree of male pronoun
dominance in the description of a hypothetical honorary position to be bestowed upon a high school
aged person, and the dependent variables are (1)
the rank assigned to a male candidate, a female
candidate and a candidate of unspecified sex, and
(2) the score given to each candidate on a checklist evaluating personal qualities which tap the
degree of sex role stereotyping to which each
candidate has been subjected (Bem 1974). Among the
groups of subjects selected to evaluate the hypothetical candidates will be:

7

1. Female undergraduates

2. Male undergraduates

3. Kiwanis Club businessmen

4. N.O.W. members

5. Male middle-aged social group members

6. Female middle-aged social group members

Next, in Chapter 4, the analysis of the experimental data yields information with which to evaluate the research questions and empirical hypotheses, and the final Chapter presents theoretical and practical implications and conclusions, as well as suggestions for further research. Having thus presented the plan of this book, the next Chapter will begin by reviewing the literature concerning the first research question.

"The limits of my language mean the limits
of my world."

> — Ludwig Wittgenstein

*   *   *

"With every language a (different) man."

> — Arab proverb

*   *   *

".   .   . a language liberates us; it
permits us to send an unlimited number of
messages and thus serves as a vehicle for
our endless thoughts. But in another sense
it enslaves us: it forces us to communicate
our thoughts in strictly regulated ways.
Does language thereby also regulate our
thoughts? Does the medium influence the
message?"

> — Moulton in _Daedalus_
> (1974)

<u>FOOTNOTES:</u> Chapter 1

[1]The McGraw-Hill guidebook which attempts to eliminate sexism from the company's publications
clearly itemizes terms and usages considered by
the editors to be injurious to children's role
conceptualization and recommendation were undertaken by the Journal of Ecumenical Studies in the
Spring of 1974, wherein it was even suggested that
the deity no longer be referred to as "He".

[2]This hypothesis states that language shapes human
conceptualizations by limiting the available cate-
gories and labels for coding experience.

[3]A new lexicon was developed by drug users not
only for concealment of illegal activity, but out
of a need for standardized terminology (Agar 1974).

[4]The following is a typical "apology" which I
have run into while reading introductions to
linguistic texts: ". . . many utterances in
English appear to result from male chauvinism
. . . rules of English dictate that <u>he</u> (and not
<u>she</u> or <u>it</u>) must be used to refer back to a sex-
ually ambiguous antecedent . . . centuries of
social convention have made <u>he</u> the acceptable
word here. Similarly, throughout this book
English has forced me to use other apparently
sexist words . . . that appear to ignore the
female sex." (Farb, pp. 7-8).

[5]The Ecumenical Council (1974) has suggested
as the most valid and useful criterion for
linguistic sexism that men should ask themselves if they would be comfortable being
referred to by the opposite sex term. For
example, would men mind being referred to by
the clergy as "sisters"? If so, then "brethren"
is a sexist term. Another insightful example
which the article provided was the word
"emasculate" which implies that only the man is
vigorous. The Ecumenical Council took the stand
that such language rests on harmful, even if
tacit, assumptions of human inequality.

[6]"Dictionary Editor" by Marguerite Beck Rex, Sun Press (Cleveland, Ohio) October 31, 1974.

[7]This hypothesis has been adopted directly from Joan Huber's introduction to Changing Women in a Changing Society (1973):

> "Men in the most highly rewarded occupations (professionals and managers) show the most hostility to change because they have the most to lose."

Such men resist any moves toward equal opportunity for women, feeling their privileges threatened and challenged.

[8]Some examples: American Psychological Associations Guidelines for Nonsexist Use of Language (June 1974); the previously footnoted McGraw-Hill guidebook, and Journal of Ecumenical Studies (both 1974); a new version of the Strong Vocational Interest Blank, designed to eliminate "subtle sexism" (July 1974).

11

Chapter 2: REVIEW OF RELEVANT LITERATURE

First Research Question: Does the degree
of male pronoun dominance in the American
English language have any effect on the
way people bestow status upon males and
females?

The empirical hypotheses associated with the
first research question, initially that standard
English is associated with pro-male biases, second-
ly that non-sexist English promotes female biases,
and lastly that English with no sex-related pronouns
induces no biases, all imply that the form and content of language develop and maintain sex roles and
biases. The male-pronoun dominance dimension, which
constitutes the independent variable in this study,
can be construed as a formal aspect of language,
rather than a contentive one. However, it seems a
worthy line of reasoning that the same way "he" is
the pronoun of choice when referring to people of
both sexes, little boys are usually the protag-
onists of literature designed for children of both
sexes, and profiles of human progress project the
male image to represent achievements of both sexes.
Whereas, use of "he" evokes formal aspects of language analysis, and use of boy-heroes, male-achiev-
ers and passive females evokes content consideration, the traditional distinctions between form and
content seem irrelevant when indeed male-dominance
is projected both ways.

Content analysis for sex biasing originated,
ironically enough, from concerns over anti-male
biases in children's texts. Suspicions that the
male image was being damaged grew out of observations that boys have far more serious problems
than girls in language-related skills in the
early elementary school grade levels.

The landmark study on how the content of
written language in American reading primers dealt
with male and female roles was conducted by Sara
Goodman Zimet (1970). It was her work which

13

attempted to document distortions of the male child image in children's literature from colonial days to the mid-1960's and to link these distortions to the excessive failure rates which American boys display in early reading acquisition. Since the boy-image was (and presumably still is) both "feminized" and immature, it was hypothesized that boys were "turned-off" by the content and in the absence of motivation and attention, failed to learn reading skills as successfully as females.

Zimet hypothesized that the content of primers was designed to amalgamate a feminized sex role for both boys and girls in the early years, probably because the feminized stereotype produces more manageable and docile students. However, Zimet suggests and other researchers have noted (Hillman 1974) that as children progress from primers to readers, and as they become more and more active in identifying with characters in stories, the sex role stereotypes emerge in highly differentiated, male-dominant themes. It is well-established that characters and plots affect ego development and conflict resolution in children as documented by Witty (1964), McClelland (1961), and most thoughtfully by Jennings (1965, p. 40). How this control is effected is usually explained in terms of identification with role models through perceived similarities between the child and the model or by observed reinforcement of behaviors depicted in the stories.

What Zimet concludes and recommends from her vast content analyses is that:

> ". . . roles for both sexes should reflect <u>what is</u> as well as <u>what should be</u>. For example, female characters would be engineers, doctors, reporters, scientist, taxi drivers, letter carriers, secretaries, teachers, nurses, and store clerks, <u>as well as</u> mothers, maiden aunts, sisters and daughters . . ."

14

and as for males, they should be depicted as:

> ". . . nurses, teachers, secretaries, cooks, waiters, store clerks, lawyers, mechanics and carpenters <u>as well as</u> fathers, bachelor uncles, brothers and sons. Inside the home, married and/or unmarried women and men would both carry out the household and/or nurturant roles in a way that would not detract from a man's competence or emphasize a woman's incompetence" (Zimet 1970, p. 138).

This highly revealing quotation, written by a woman with a doctorate, expresses both a belief that the content of language exerts great control over children, and a covert frustration about the content of the written language of her youth. Recommending models of androgynous households hints at the obstacles she has avoided or overcome in her unusally high climb for achievement. But what Zimet seems to have overlooked is the built-in linguistic <u>weltanshaungs</u> which are not overcome simply by casting a woman as a doctor or a welder, and a man as a nurse or secretary. The characterizations persist in the following manner.

Users of language tend to say "he is a <u>male</u> nurse: or I have "a <u>woman</u> doctor" because language encodes <u>and</u> perpetuates deeply rooted stereotypes wherein the plain usage of doctor implies male, just as nurse implies female. Furthermore, according to Horner (1972), in real life <u>male</u> secretaries rarely make the coffee for their bosses, and <u>women</u> doctors deal far more frequently with family and personal (almost nurturant) matters than in pure research or extremely skilled domains (e.g., surgery). Therefore, how much "progress" has actually occurred simply by scrambling sex and job titles?

The obvious answer, that only little progress has occurred, can be harmonized with the chorus of all the social sciences, whose refrains serve to remind us that change is always slow when large groups of people and institutions are involved. So the content of language persists in transmitting stereotypes even when deliberate attempts are made to reduce stereotyping because words carry connotations and auras beyond the control of the speaker or writer.

Another way that the content of language develops and maintains sex roles besides providing stereotypes is by not providing terms for certain realities, thereby relegating those realities to non-legitimized or incommunicable status. For example, what is the exact term for a male nymphomaniac? Another rather humorous example was provided by Jane Otten in Newsweek (December 30, 1974, p. 9), when she pondered various terms to refer to the man with whom her daughter was cohabiting. "Son-in-common-law" was explicit but did not fit the bill; "lover-in-law" sounded like a meaningful relationship with the parent of a spouse; "roommate," "suitor," "boyfriend," consort" and everything else she mentioned either said too much or too little, "son-out-law" was merely good for a laugh. The absence of a usable term, except within very intimate circles, for people involved in cohabitation relationships signals the violation of norms and is itself a social sanction.

Another conspicuous absence in the content of our language which contributes to the acquisition and maintenance of sex roles is the lack of a neuter singular personal pronoun. Because we (and many other linguistic communities) lack this part of speech, either "he" or "she" must be used, since "it" is considered derogatory when referring to humans (except babies). The fact that "he" has always been the pronoun of choice does convey a message to people as they use language. The message in 1975 as expressed in popular media, e.g. Marlo Thomas' record and book Free To Be . . . You and Me, Ms. Magazine, radio and TV spots (Jacklin and Mischel 1973), and newspapers, seems to be that girls as young as six years old are sensitized to and offended by assumptions of masculine gender. Appendix A summarizes pilot studies conducted in preparation for this literature review which document young girls' reactions to male dominated language.

The mechanism through which male pronoun and image dominance may develop and maintain sex roles could involve covert discriminative stimuli. In keeping with the Pavlovian paradigm of language as a "second signal system," a conditioning procedure may occur when language is experienced in a context of constant pairing of maleness and positive attributes, and femaleness and negative or less positive attributes. This procedure can suppress behaviors which are not reinforced by language pairing, or promote frequently associated pairs, such that the semantic content can acquire excitatory or inhibitory properties which govern basic human tendencies. If language "favors" the male person, then this preferential treatment can potentially account for some sex differences like the one presented here: Kagan and Moss (1962) found that "the typical female has greater anxiety over aggressive and competitive behavior than the male. She, therefore, experiences greater conflict over intellectual competition which in turn leads to inhibition of intense strivings for academic excellence." This early finding has been updated by studies compiled in Maccoby (1974, p. 155) and Horner (1972).

The use of "he/she" or even "she" half the time when describing generalized achievement situations may alter associational links between sex and attributes, thereby changing expectations which have been socially implicit, thereby encouraging (perhaps by disinhibition) achievement in females. The anxiety of norm violations would be eliminated, and perhaps this is what "women's lib" has recognized as a focal concern: women's potentials must be released from cultural inhibitions.

Bardwick (1971, p. 181) illustrates an amusing and typical case of competitive hostessing among bridge players, which can be viewed as disinhibition of repressed behavior patterns. I interpret her depiction as an example of how when given a situation where achievements are always linked with feminine pronouns, females strive as unabashedly as males in their designated areas. The "she" consistently associated with cooking and baking "excites" or releases food preparation behaviors in women toward which they can "cathect" their productive energy. Implicit in this suggestion is the speculation that if typical male activities were suddenly linked consistently with "she" when speaking to today's infants, females would grow up striving for excellence in traditionally masculine realms.

A study by E. Paul Torrance (1960) demonstrated a similar speculation, that females may be suffering from normatively repressed creativity. On the first task he administered to pre-adolescent children, boys were twice as creative as girls. After a pep talk with parents and teachers designed to encourage the girls, another equivalent task was given. Girls scored just as well as boys; however, both boys and girls still evaluated the boys' performance much higher. A simple adjustment in the tacit expectations, a clear invitation to girls for them to strive and to create, significantly affected the girls' performance. Self-image was not as accessible to modification as was performance, but perhaps as a result of repeated successful performances, females would adjust their self-evaluation.

Thus far, sex-related differences in school achievement have been linked to the content of language by Zimet (1970) insofar as little boys are repelled by early feminized stereotypes, and later, girls are subjugated by male-dominant form, characters, themes and associations in both written and spoken spheres. Basil Bernstein, when analyzing similar problems of poor school performance related to socioeconomic status, stated that the form of language limits one's capabilities in many important ways:

". . . it is reasonable to argue that the genes of social class may well be carried not through a genetic code but through a communication code that social class itself promotes. Whereas this code may be okay everywhere else, it makes for trouble in school . . .

18

". . . different speech systems or codes
create for their speakers different orders
of relevance and relation. . . As the child
learns his speech, or in the terms I shall
use here, learns specific codes which regulate his verbal acts, he learns the requirements of his social structure. . . From this
point of view, every time the child speaks
or listens (or reads), the social structure
is reinforced in him and his social identity
shaped" (Bernstein 1972, pp. 472-73)."

Though Bernstein was addressing issues of class-
linked thought and language patterns, he could not
have illustrated more clearly sex biases in expression which may also shape children's social identi-
ties. Society seems to reinforce maleness.
Femaleness is also imposed via social contingencies.
Analogizing from class to sex, "femininity" may be
transmitted linguistically to girls as well as via
the XX chromosome formation.

If one claims that sexism in language suppresses
and oppresses females, then it is necessary to demonstrate that either males and females use language
differently, or that females and males are spoken
and written to and about differently, or all of the
above. Just as Bernstein based his claim on documented socioeconomic differentials in language
usage (1972, p. 474), documentation of male and
female languages in all of the above senses will
be established below; therefore, sufficient differences in language exist for it to be a perpetuating force for sex roles.

Documentation of male and female language forms
is as follows: Warshaw (1972) found that men use
more verbs, more power-associated adjectives, whereas females use more nouns, more reference to inner
states; Barron's (1971) data reinforce Warshaw's,
also indicating general grammatical sex-linked
preferences. Bossard (1945) notes that ". . . linguistic variations occur along whatever role and
status dimensions a society may employ to distin-
guish various segments within itself." He contin-

19

ues by observing that family table talk is sex appropriate, that language is enforced in terms of tone of voice, volume, diction, intensity, stock phrases, habits of exclamation and subjects discussed and tabooed.

Not only do males and females generate different styles of English, but they are characterized differently by members of both sexes. McClelland (1965) has concluded from his data that females are perceived and defined as the opposite of men -- and the adjectives describing men are all positive ones. Both sexes describe men as "large," "strong," "hard," "heavy." Bardwick (1971) augments McClelland's data with the findings that the opposite adjectives which characterize females are "small," "weak," "soft," and "light." The female image also includes the adjectives "dull," "peaceful," "relaxed," "cold," "rounded," "passive" and "slow." Value judgments of "male equals superior" and "female equals inferior" are consistently found in the social sciences (Bardwick 1965; Clifford 1973; Walstar 1971).

To sum up, language is used by people of both sexes to characterize those sexes differentially, with obvious devaluation of "feminine" characteristics. Not only that, but the very purpose of language may vary by sex. Women use speech patterns to indicate their status, whereas men are judged by their jobs and income. Therefore, controlling for class, women use speech forms associated with more prestigious education and socioeconomic levels than men (Farb 1972, p. 50).

Labov (1972) has noted a greater sensitivity to slight variations in language among women than among men, which harmonizes with Farb's previous observation, since if language matters more to women than to men, women would be more likely to notice minor characteristics. Lakoff (1975) has outlined detailed sex differences in language usage on the levels of intonation, frequency of form of sentences (interrogatives, imperatives, declaratives, etc.), syntax (women use tag questions for verification at the end of sentences, e.g., "isn't it?" and "right?" and women hedge more, e.g., "sort of," "in my opinion") and at the level of words (women use many evaluative terms, e.g., "really," "precious," "divine").

The degree to which there exist male and female languages, and the effect of such differentiation should be assessed by much more comprehensive and vigorous investigations. Content analyses and survey data do not yield explanatory information and remain purely descriptive. Thus far, all that can be safely concluded is that males and females do use language differently, and are referred to differently and preferentially by users of language. Therefore, language could be involved in the formation and maintenance of sex roles.

Although appeals to authority could be made in the realms of psychology, sociology, philosophy and linguistics[10] for the opinion that language helps effect stereotyping, what is needed is evidence and explanation rather than speculation. This study's first research question and associated empirical hypotheses attempt to gather such evidence. Despite the compelling, always appreciable logic of Roger Brown in the following selection, some estimation of the actual impact of linguistic "sexism" on the socialization of sex roles in people is needed.

> "Because words have symbolic properties, because their usage is patterned with reference to the total environment, language can cause a cognitive structure. To the degree that children are motivated to speak a language as it is spoken in their community they are motivated to share the world view of that community" (Brown 1970, p. 242).

Available labels affect our organization of reality. Words alert us to entities before we know their definitions, cause us to ask "what does that word mean?" since indeed all words have meanings. But all languages limit these meanings. International

21

interpreters attest to the complexity of language barriers which often turn out to be <u>thought</u> barriers (Glenn 1954). Professionals rely on technical language to convey economically and accurately complex realms of meaning, to isolate their trades and to prevent lay people from infiltrating or functioning competently in their areas of expertise. Official languages of multi-lingual countries are often purposely limited to the elite, to keep most citizens ignorant and "in their place" (Brameld 1969, p. 241). All the above examples illustrate the controlling and shaping properties of language and the deliberate usage of these properties to manipulate social systems. Intuition urges that this undoubtedly goes on between the sexes, but while intuition urges, data is diffident.

"A woman with ideas and the ability to express them is something of a social embarrassment, like an unhousebroken pet." (Mannes 1963)

*   *   *

"Language represents reality like a map represents territory." (Korzybski 1948)

*   *   *

"The fact is that language merely reflects social behavior and is not the cause of it. The problem of women's status in English-speaking communities will not be solved by dismantling the language -- but by changing the social structure." (Farb 1974)

23

Second Research Question: Does the degree
or role rigidity which a person displays
have any effect on the way this person
bestows status upon males and females?

The empirical hypotheses associated with this
second main research question propose positive relationships between Role Rigidity Scale scores and
pro-male biases (or anti-female biases). Additionally, evaluation of associations between other role-
related subject variables and sex biases, insofar
as they moderate the effect of the treatment on the
criterion is proposed. Finally, affiliates of
N.O.W. are identified as a group likely to demonstrate that role conceptualizations can override
the effects of sexism in language because this
group will always display pro-female bias under
all experimental conditions.

The mechanisms through which role conceptualizations can influence language and communication
presuppose trait-type approaches to psychology
wherein relatively stable personality characteristics (such as sex roles) serve as valid predictors
of behavior (language production and interpretation
of meaning). Language as overt behavior is one of
the accepted ways of considering the symbolic function in humans. Another way of viewing language is
Vygotsky's (1962). He views language as funda-
mentally internal, like thought, and as such,
largely inaccessible to direct, controlled study.

In Malenowski's (1923) conceptualization of
language, language is indeed a mode of action, not
a "countersign of thought." When viewed as action
or overt behavior, language usage becomes subject
to modification by environmental contingencies,
and can be associated with specific personality
types. The clearest evidence that roles can and
do influence language is the fact that each of us
has mastered several styles of communication which
we differentially employ depending upon our current
role. In the role of professional, we upgrade our
syntax, diction and elocution; while "rapping" we
relax and actually avoid formerly preferred words

24

and constructions; when talking to an infant we radically adapt to the role of teacher.

Since written and spoken language usage <u>are</u> behaviors and therefore, subject to environmental contingencies, the interpretation of meaning requires knowledge of the cultural and situational contexts which are part of those contingencies. The degree to which sex of language users provides us with a cultural and situational context is one answer to the question of how sex roles influence language.

There are two ways that sex roles may influence language; by affecting the production of language, and the interpretation of meaning, that is to say sex roles may affect both transmission and reception of signals. The literature review directed at the previous research question of how language shapes sex roles covers the data that males and females do generate different styles of English, each style associated with different statuses, though it does not address the degree to which sex roles determine these differences. Following the treatment of this point, the remainder of this section will treat sex roles as affecting the interpretation of meaning, creating the biases inherent in sex role-related interpretations which would lead to the results hypothesized under the second research question.

ROLES AFFECT LANGUAGE PRODUCTION

"Writing as a researcher," "speaking as a woman" and "talking as a friend" are all stock phrases used to indicate clearly that one's perceived role will be governing one's communications. Bernstein (1961, 1964) explores the hypothesis that social relationships act as "intervening variables between linguistic structures and their realization in speech." Relationships can be conceptualized as determined by role prescriptions. When large age differences exist between two people, for example, the younger usually addresses the elder with a title before the last name, <u>because</u> role prescriptions require that respect be ascribed to the elder. This seems evident because when roles change as intimacy develops, titles can be dropped just as other aspects of language relax every time formal role relationships slide into casual ones.

The theorist who most clearly attributes differentials in language production to socialization is Basil Bernstein. His distinctions between elaborated vs. restricted codes, and person vs. object modes are described chiefly through social class variations, but many of the principles seem to apply to sex as well as class. Females can be observed to have a tendency toward generating elaborated and person-oriented codes, while males would tend to generate restricted, object-oriented codes (Kramer 1974, Oakoff 1975, Warshaw 1971). In other words, women generally expand upon thoughts and focus more upon people and feelings than men do.

Sex roles as causes of these different codes can be explained as follows: "an elaborated code arises out of a social relationship where the intent of the other person cannot be taken for granted" (Deutscher 1967, p. 53). Therefore, through the use of extensive verbal expression, thoughts and intentions are clarified. Women, granted less credibility, would theoretically feel required to elaborate their ideas more thoroughly to combat the basic lack of confidence granted to them. Comparing this to restricted codes,

> "The use of a restricted code creates social solidarity at the cost of the verbal elaboration of individual experience . . . An elaborated code will arise whenever the culture or subcultural emphasizes the "I" over the "we". It will arise whenever the intent of the other person cannot be taken for granted" (Bernstein 1972, p. 476).

The early distinctions between elaborated vs. restricted codes were accompanied by far-reaching value judgments and social class associations. The restricted code was linked with low SES, poor academic performance and impoverished conceptualization. More recently (Bernstein 1972), the distinction among usages of the two codes has been clarified; all socioeconomic groups use all varieties of restricted and elaborated codes, but in varying social contexts for specific interpersonal aims. For example, unique and personal experiences or insights seem to require elaborated codes, including novel expressions and "unpredictable syntax" (Bernstein's terms).

Along Bernstein's clarified notion of differential usage of elaborated and restricted coding, then, the feminist pressure toward explicit inclusion of females in generic statements about people may bespeak the novel experiences and insights of women who are expanding their horizons and wish to communicate their new actualizations to present and future members of society.

Distrust as well as a desire to communicate novel experience may motivate many feminists to object to male dominance in English. The premise that "he" can be used to stand for all people may be interpreted as restricted in code, and appropriate only within intimate communities with shared values. "He/she" or "person" rather than "man" prefixes and suffixes represent the elaborated code, and are free from room for interpretation, therefore less dependent upon shared values and communality of roles exist to allow male-designated generic references. This attitude itself defines a role of social progressivism which generates its own language. Then, in turn,

> "The language of social protest, with its challenging of assumptions, its grasping toward new cultural forms, may play an important role in breaking down the limitations of subculturally bound restricted

codes" (referring to Civil Rights Movement, Bernstein, p. 493).

The full circle of language, resulting from special roles, and then in turn perpetuating and developing these special roles is complete. If any point of entry into the cycle is to be found, it is probably at the point where individuals creatively develop innovations in their roles, which generate new elements in language usage, which then influence adjacent roles along the themes expressed in the novel language. Bernstein (1972, p. 479) speculates that if roles change and language codes do not, the result will be strain born of suppressed expression. Clearly at this point of strain many women seek relief by joining discussion groups to share their awarenesses with other women who also suffer strain. Together they learn to express their new consciousness.[11]

"New cultural processes require new symbols. But often these symbols are, for a time at least, unavailable. Conflict and distortion result from the fact that old symbolic systems are retained and applied to events, beliefs, institutions, and attitudes for which they were never intended" (Brameld, p. 254).

The response to this void in language for the women's movement was first to expose the constraints placed upon women's roles, then to parallel this with an expose' on sexism in language as part of the above constraints and as an effect of the history of male dominance.

". . . girls learn to be feminine (to) take cues from authoritative males . . . catering to people's palates, to their moods, to their needs -- these are feminine skills . . ." (Angrist 1969, p. 230).

And the production of language by women reflects these role prescriptions with the highest frequency of women's language content focused on describing feelings and interpersonal relationships while men stress actions and achievements. The situation in Burundi is no different in form, as the following account illustrates:

> "The norms governing the uses of speech are explicitly differentiated according to caste, sex, and age so that the relations of speech behavior to sociological structure are easily grasped by observers . . . Girls in the upper caste are carefully trained, but to artful silence and evasiveness and careful listening that will enable them to repeat nearly verbatim what has been said by visitors and neighbors" (Albert 1972, pp. 74, 77).

In the Burundi culture, then, part of the feminine role requires a very specific and, by American standards, deviant language usage. A woman behaving "properly" for the Burundi culture would probably be hospitalized here as a result of her bizarre language behavior. In fact, numerous studies have shown that even within our culture, what is evaluated as feminine is often also evaluated as mentally defective. For example, Broverman et al. (1970) experimented with sets of behaviors which subjects classified as "female" and found that these same behaviors were classified as mentally unhealthy by the same members of our culture. Therefore, women are socialized into and defined in terms of mental capabilities which the culture evaluates as inferior. No wonder the language generated by women has been judged as less mature and accurate (Stone and Church 1972). Childlike, subordinate qualities are what many men desire in a woman. They are part of the female role prescriptions which may influence women's language production.

One-third of college men interviewed by Huber (1971) could not cope with hypothetical situations of female intellectual superiority as recently as 1970. The men's strain and withdrawal from superior females hurt the men as much as it did the women, since the norm of male intellectual superiority is hard to live up to and causes men much discomfort. Therefore, further speculation (Yerby 1974) indicates high rates of role change will be demonstrated by men who interact frequently with high-achieving women in an attempt by these men to minimize inferiority feelings.

Many women, aware of the traditional judgments and expectations concerning femininity, consciously and subconsciously alter their communication strategies when trying to appeal to men in order to be less threatening and more "feminine." Role prescriptions, awesomely powerful in shaping all manners of behavior, seem to influence language productions along "sex-appropriate" lines, and what remains to be explored is the effect of sex roles on the interpretation of meaning.

ROLES AFFECT THE INTERPRETATION OF MEANING

"The meaning language conveys cannot be divorced from the behavioral context in which it orignates or in which it is used" (Kimball 1974, p. v). Roles can be considered vital factors involved in the context from which language originates, but again, a grand statement of theory cannot substitute for data. Ervin-Tripp (1969) displays how social relations limit language, and she does so by amassing empirical observations. Finding that people in relationships act selectively on what, when and how things are said, it appears that the form of a social relation regulates options for language use at both syntactic and lexical levels.

Studies replicated in Canada, Wales, the U.S.A. and many other countries consistently demonstrate how interpretation of meaning is influenced by perceptions of the role of the speaker (Callary 1974). Using a matched-guise technique, tapes are prepared by one speaker varying his accent, first simulating a member of the dominant group, then a minority member. Subjects judge the speaker and never

fail to differentiate broadly, based on role stereotyping alone, which "speaker" (actually which
guise) is more serious, more credible or more
interesting.

Perceived inequality in speakers affects the
attention they pay to each other, the credibility
extended and the impact of the message. Basic
field theory in perception such as Brunswik's
(1956) predicts that knowledge of social roles
should greatly influence what one hears when a role
member speaks because the probabilistics of diction
and syntax are limited by the perceived role of the
speaker.

The classic illustration of how roles influence meaning is offered by Kochman (1974) when he
notes that "Lyndon Johnson need not change his
accent to become President, but a black (often)
must do so to get an ordinary job." Accents similar to L.B.J.'s in blacks connote undesirable
attributes in the minds of whites (and perhaps many
blacks, too) and the accent is interpreted totally
in light of the role and identity of the speaker.
In other words, a Southern drawl means something
different coming from the oval office of the White
House than it does from a black person desiring to
rent an apartment. Words, too, are interpreted
differently depending on the perceived roles of the
message sender and receiver. Ambiguities are
resolved by summoning up extraneous information,
usually involving the role and status of the
speaker. Abstracting one step further, there is
meaning in the observance of linguistic rules and
conventions, just as there is meaning in the violation of communication norms (Gottman 1956,
p. 475). These meanings can only be construed by
considering the source of violations or observan-
ces.

Empirical evidence for the above assertions
comes from basic psychology (perceptual "sets"
engendered by roles), from psycholinguistics (Bruce
1956), and sociolinguistics (Labov 1966). Gumperz
(1972) discusses meanings within the context of

roles when he asks the questions: What meanings are associated with the language styles available to us from which we select what we will use? What is the relationship between the type of language selected and the situation of the choice? These questions are most commonly answered by inferring the purpose of the message from the total context.[12] Labov (1966, 1970, 1972) collected data and analyzed it several times to explore the meaning of phonetic variants of speech in certain contexts. Though he clearly identified meanings attributed to speakers by listeners based on slight regional accents, the speakers did not voluntarily choose to speak in a particular way. Their accents were usually beyond their awareness and control. However, listeners <u>did</u> embue auditory patterns with status, credibility and interest valences, all of which affect interpretation of meaning, whether intended or unintended by the speaker. At this semantic level, similar styles of selecting linguistic alternatives emerge and contribute to the interpretation process.

Semantics, the realm of linguistics dealing specifically with meaning, has often been considered the study of how ambiguities are resolved.[13] Hardly a sentence can be generated that is not full of ambiguities. For example, in the sentence you just read, "sentence" could be a grammatical term or a pronouncement of a court of law. "Hardly" could mean "with difficulty" or "almost never." Since ambiguities are constantly resolved in light of context, and roles are part of the social context, roles of the message sender and receiver influence the interpretation of meaning.

Looking ahead, in terms of the experiment to be described in the next chapter, hypothetical candidates will be evaluated by subjects. A person who conceives of roles in traditional, inflexible terms should evaluate the candidates along a pro-male predisposition in keeping with the well established norms and personal values of our culture, despite the style of language used to describe the honorary position for which the candidates are competing. However, people possessing liberal, flexible role attitudes should interpret the descriptive language of the honorary position in line with their progressive pre-dispositions, thereby responding to the treatment effects as designed. This means that for people with moderate role rigidity, therefore, language effects should appear as predicted. The next chapter will explore how imposed modifications of language could influence attitudes.

"There is no more reason for language to change than there is for automobiles to add fins one year and remove them the next."

                            - Postal (1968)

          *   *   *

"Language is the litmus paper of culture."

                            - Guralnik (1974)

          *   *   *

Semantic depletion is a significant form of language change, wherein communicative power is stripped from a word, leaving mainly evocative power. For example:
Atomic Bomb   Atomic Energy Commission
Atomic Dry Cleaners   Atomic Music Company.

Is "man" in the generic sense a totally depleted term?

Third Research Question: What effect would
the condition of non-sexist English have on
the way people bestow status upon males and
females?

The empirical hypotheses associated with the
third research question, that Kiwanis Club members
and middle age subjects will tend to backlash under
the non-sexist treatment condition, i.e. increase
their preferences for the male candidate, rely on
some speculation about how language changes in
relation to cultural attitudes and values. The
assumption being tested is that conservative,
traditional groups of people will resist imposed,
progressive language change by responding in a
reactionary fashion. Implied is that more natural processes of gradual change may not elicit
the backlash, or reactionary response, and that
indeed the intentions of feminist language reform-
ers may be counteracted by their recommendations
for imposed language change.

Prudence dictates that the processes of language change, official and unofficial, regarding
written and spoken modalities, be explored, and
empirical observation of people's reactions be
obtained prior to recommending or enforcing arti-
ficially imposed changes. Lexicography is the
most obvious source for primary exploration of language change.

The official authorities for language change
are the creators of dictionaries and compilers of
grammatical and syntactical rules. Zgusta Ladislov,
author of the Manual of Lexicography (1971), admits
that language usage changes far too quickly for
lexicographers to keep up with current trends.
Therefore, the categorization of words as "obsolete,"
"obsolescent," "archaic," "informal," "slang,"
"taboo," "dialetical," "formal," "standard," "joc-
ular", "literal," "hyperbolic" and so on may be
outdated before lexicographies come off the press.

For this reason at least, lexicographers seem
to wish that they were not revered as ultimate

authorities. Dictionaries seem to be intended primarily for descriptive, not prescriptive, functions
but are used with the opposite goals in mind.

Failure to keep up with changes in semantics
and grammar may reflect the inherent nature of
human language more than the shortcomings of lexicography. However, one area in which lexicography
seems clearly wanting is in the explicit statement
of criteria for determining synonymy, connotations
and denotations. The standards used to decide how
popular a usage has to be before it is accepted are
never explicated. Furthermore, it is never clear
who the target group of the dictionary is, either
geographically, professionally or culturally.
Finally, lexicographers should address the problems
of written vs. spoken language. Without explica-
ting all of the above, it is most difficult to
explore official channels of language change.

Ferguson (1971) addresses the problem of written vs. spoken language by commenting that "Linguists
like to point out that speech is primary and writing secondary and that written language is always
in some sense a representation of speech . . .
(however, Ferguson claims that) . . . written language frequently develops characteristics not found
in the corresponding spoken language . . . the
existence of a written variety inhibits language
change" and has higher status, as if writing is
"real" English and speech is the corruption of it.
Therefore, writing is subject to careful analysis
and legislated change, whereas speech is more
"natural," basic and uncontrollable. In accordance
with this phenomenon, all the aforementioned guidelines for elimination of sexism in language have
restricted themselves to the written modes of
expression.

What emerges is an immediate reversal of natural processes of language change. Since the written mode is most accessible to enforcement of
guidelines, it is the object of guidelines. Yet
written language retains the most conservative,
formal constraints which "proper usage" dictates.

Writing cannot contain liberal slang, informal constructions or experimental, tentative usages. Normally, those avant-garde explorations in change are tested out in the spoken mode of expression, and if they pass the tests of time and popularity, they ascend into the domain of written language.

That written language inhibits change is certainly important interpersonally. Offensive statements are better said than written, since they can be forgotten or contradicted, but the permanence and irrefutability of written messages is forbidding. The main relevance of distinguishing between spoken and written language here is that politically-oriented programs promoting specific language changes have far more dramatic effects on the written mode than on spoken language. This reversal of apparently natural processes of language change may indeed accelerate evolution of language but it also may cause resistance, hostility and even backlash effects in certain segments of the population. Thus, the ridicule of feminist terms such as "Ms." and "personhood" when used in speech seems to exceed the negative reactions to those terms when used in writing, because guidelines and recommendations have been circulating that govern written usage, while few official attempts have been made to influence conversation.

The previously cited McGraw-Hill guidelines for Equal Treatment of the Sexes provides basic recommendations which were followed in this study's experimental treatment termed "non-sexist English." The existence of backlash effects can be examined, since the non-sexist condition would result in an augmented preference for the male candidate if backlashing were occurring. Such findings would be evidence that change which is imposed too suddenly is rejected. The motivation which would account for a particular population backlashing can be deduced from recent parallels with racism. Any trend enabling women to compete equally with men sets off a defensive fear of loss, both of status and money, reminiscent of white people's fears of Affirmative Action programs. The backlash response is an attempt to shut out competition.

While certain written language can be subject to guidelines, requirements, and even legislation, much more subtle dynamics are involved in speech. In the natural process of linguistic change, low-prestige language is subjected to hypercorrection by peers (Labov 1972, Chapt. 5), and the precise mechanisms of changes are delineated throughout Labov's book, Sociolinguistic Patterns:

> "The Neo-grammarian viewpoint is that such observable shifts (in pronuonciation) are the results of a series of borrowings, imitations, and random variations. At the first stage of change where linguistic changes originate, we may observe many sporadic side-effects of articulation pro-cesses which have no linguistic meaning; no socially determined significance is attached to them, either in the differing of morpheme, or in expressive function. Only when social meaning is assigned to such variation will they be imitated and begin to play a role in the language. Regularity is then to be found in the end result of the process. . . not in the beginning" (Labov 1972, pp. 23-24).

At the level of phonemes, linguistic changes seem to be random or at best, whimsical. Postal (1968, p. 283) comments "There is no more reason for languages to change than there is for automo-biles to add fins one year and remove them the next." Yet Labov clearly points out in the passage above that systematic change only occurs at the level of morphemes or higher, and then those sounds associated with social significance get imitated, indicating far more social relevance of language change than Postal is willing to do.

Though a great deal of language changes may be insidious and beyond social awareness, Postal's statement imparts a purposelessness and frivolous-ness which misrepresents the impact of linguistic change. More accurately, "Languages undergo development when their functions undergo real or anticipatory expansion as a result of the expanded role repertoires (once more, real or anticipated) of those for whom those languages have become too symbolic of group membership and group goals to be easily displaced" (Fishman 1968, p. 9). Certainly, women today are experiencing expanded role repertoires, yet are still communicating with language that symbolizes outdated sex category characteristics and goals. Therefore, despite the fact that Fishman was concentrating on bilingual cultures his remarks fit the experience of today's women's movement.

Even though there are pressures being exerted by feminists to eliminate "sexism" in languages, it is possible that pressures toward elimination of male pronoun dominance from the English language are symptoms of excessive reification on the part of sexism-sensitive groups.[14] In other words, it is important to be sure that male pronoun dominance is more than a trivial figure of speech before one tries to institute language reforms. Information processing theory speaks of signals, noise, channels, code and message, and how important it is that signals be distinguished from noise. The question is: Are "sexist" terms signals to users of our language or are they nothing more than noise, with no socializing or detrimental effects?

The experiment described in this book will address the above question through a design which tests the three research hypotheses from several aspects: the style of language (degree of male pronoun dominance) and its effect on sex biases; role rigidity and its effect on sex biases; and, the stimulus value of non-sexist English as an agent for linguistic change. The following Chapter describes the methodology for collecting the data, securing the subjects, compiling the instruments and executing the procedure.

[9]Specific parts of speech and vocabulary words
are not the only areas demonstrating voids for
women's concerns. Among the "sexist sins of
omission" the literature search has revealed
a telling obliviousness to the topic of sexism in language. The finding is consistent
with the failure to study sexism throughout
the social sciences. Ironically in Coleman's
(1969, pp. 105-6) expose' of "research lacunae"
in social science, Coleman himself fails to
note that among the negelected areas of study
is sexism. Language and Language Behavior
Abstracts, to cite a glaring example, has a
grand total of three entries in its 1974
indices under headings of sex, gender, roles,
male, female or women. The years through 1980
are similarly sparse.

[10]The Whorfian hypothesis of linguistic relativism
is the best-known theory that stresses the control which our language has over our concepts.
Restated more clearly by Bernstein (1972), it
puts forth that:

   ". . . embedded in a culture or subculture
may be a basic organizing concept, concepts,
or themes whose ramifications may be diffused
throughout the culture or subculture. The
speech forms through which the culture or
subculture is realized transmits this organizing concept or concepts within their ges-
talt rather than through any set of meanings."

In the original, Whorf stated that language "is
not merely a reproducing instrument for voicing
ideas but rather is itself the shaper of ideas."

[11]Consciousness-raising is the "name given to the
feminist practice or examining one's personal
experience in the light of sexism, i.e., that
theory which explains women's subordinate position in sociology as a result of a cultural

decision to confer direct power on men and only indirect power on women: (Gornick 1971).

[12]Dell Hymes in the introduction to Cazden (1972, p. iii) has written:

> "What is crucial is not so much a better understanding of how language is struc-tured, but a better understanding of how language is used; not so much what lan-guage is, as what language is for.   Lin-guists have generally taken questions of use and purpose for granted.   They have not related the structure of language to the structure of speaking."

[13]James Joyce in Portrait of the Artist as a Young Man, defined language brilliantly as "ambiguiti_s probing ambiguities."

[14]Symbols must not be confused with the realities they symbolize -- that symbols have no objective force or existence of their own but are simply tolls that man (sic!) has fashioned for explain-ing and controlling his environment" (Brameld 1959, p. 256).

41

Chapter 3:   Methodology for Data Collection

SUBJECTS:

Subjects have been obtained representing six populations: undergraduate males, undergraduate females, Kiwanis Club businessmen, affiliates of the National Organization for Women, and middle-aged and elderly church social group members, both male and female.   There are thirty-six subjects per group, twelve per experimental condition within each group, making up a total of 216 people.

These subjects are described in terms of their age, sex, level of education, occupation (current or future), religion, degree of religiosity, social class, expectations of socioeconomic mobility and Role Rigidity scores (see Appendix B).   In all six groups, the subjects were members of classes or clubs whose leaders or teachers allowed me to approach them during a meeting to ask their cooperation in my study.   Participation required twenty to thirty minutes, after which subjects were debriefed and an explanation of my work provided them with a program for their meeting.

The 216 subjects were distilled from a grand total of 257 who were approached; 17 left part of their responses blank and were therefore rejected as incomplete; 12 politely asked to spectate rather than to participate; and another 12 were randomly eliminated before they were scored because they were above and beyond the predetermined number of subjects required for the design.   In all classes of people approached but not participating (incompletes, spectators and excesses), distribution was not clustered in any of the groups of subjects, inducing no systematic bias on that basis.

Subjects' questions and thoughtful contributions, in the debriefing and discussion program which I provided following data collection, were most helpful in interpreting some of the group effects which emerged in the analysis.

43

PROCEDURE

Description of Treatments

The treatment consisted of the style of English used to describe an honorary position for which the subjects were selecting a candidate. The conditions were:

1. Standard English (using male pronouns);

2. Non-sexist English (using "he/she," "she/he" and "person" instead of "man"):

3. Neutral English (itemized description without any pronouns).

After reading the description, subjects evaluated three candidates, a male, a female and an unspecified person. Subjects completed an adaptation of the Bem (1974) Sex Role Inventory for each of the three candidates; next they indicated their order preferences for the position of world youth delegate, and finally they completed a brief questionnaire about themselves. This information provided criterion data about how the style of English employed to describe the position (the treatment) affected the relative evaluation of candidates (the criterion) controlling for all variables except the sex of candidates.

Each subject received an eight-page protocol (see Appendix C) the first page being a general orienting paragraph.[15] Page 2 was the experimental treatment, a presentation of one of the three following levels of male pronoun dominance:

Treatment 1 -- Male Pronoun Dominant English (Standard English)

"You have been asked to help select a delegate to the First International World Youth Conference. Selection from among outstanding high school students has already been done by distinguised teachers,

44

councilmen and clergymen, narrowing the field to three candidates. Your final selection should be made on the basis of four qualities that join to form a whole person:

1. Concern for mankind --

   The applicant should view his life as an opportunity for serving his fellow man beyond his own personal interests.

2. Intellectual excellence --

   The applicant's grade point average should reflect his ability to apply himself and to achieve highly. The range of subjects of interest to him should be broad and flexible.

3. Social disposition and patriotism --

   The applicant should show evidence of working well with others, such as sportsmanship, chairmanship of clubs and committees, or person-oriented hobbies, and be active in civic, democratic, American past-times.

4. Concern for broad ethical or religious values and social responsibility --

   Note that these qualities may take any of several forms, depending on the background of the individual applicant and the particular stage of his life which he has reached at the time of application. He may or may not be a participating member of a religious denomination; he will often be wrestling with the problems of the relationship between his concerns and the ideas generated by serious scholarship; he may have found the institutionalized form of religion unsatisfactory

and may be in rebellion against it,
or he may have found strength through
active participation in his church or
synagogue.

Finally, and above all, the delegate should
be someone you would be proud to have represent America and to promote the brotherhood
of man. Please read the candidates' qualifications carefully and score them quickly,
as first impressions are most reliable."

An alternative page 2, which one-third of the
subjects (at random) received was the second experimental treatment, the non-sexist condition.
Although there potentially are numerous ways to
eliminate male pronoun dominance, the one used in
my study represents the actual changes put forth
most frequently by the majority of guidelines and
legislators in our country. Thus, my non-sexist
treatment represents actual language reforms as
opposed to mere possibilities.

Treatment 2 -- Non-Sexist English

Paragraph 1 -- Change "councilmen" to "members
of Council," "clergyman" to "members of
clergy."

First Quality -- Change "mankind" to "humani-
ty," change all instances of "his" to "his/
her" alternating with "her/his," change
"his fellow man" to "all people."

Second Quality -- Change "his" to "her/his"
alternating with "his/her" (even him/herself).

Third Quality -- Change "sportsmanship" to
"teamwork," "Chairmanship" to "the chairing
of."

Fourth Quality -- Change "his" and "him" as
previously directed, also "he" to "he/she"
or "she/he", change "brotherhood of man"
to "family of all peoples."

The third treatment is a control condition
which eliminates pronouns linked to either sex.
Such a condition allows for sex-biases that are
unrelated to language to emerge, either as a function of subjects' group membership or some organismic variable like age, Role Rigidity score, education or religiosity. This itemized or telegraphic
language style is not novel or obtrusive, and should
reduce confounding of variables in group by treatment by candidate interactions. Accordingly, one-
third of the total subjects will receive page 2
along this format:

Treatment 3 -- Control, Itemized English

Paragraph 1 -- Change "teachers, councilmen
and clergymen" to "people." The other four
qualities are reworded as follows:

I.   Views life as opportunity for
      serving others beyond own per-
      sonal interests.

II.   Intellectual excellence.
         High grade point average and
       · board scores.
         Broad interest in subjects.
         Flexibility.

III. Social disposition and patriotism.
         Works well with others, e.g.,
         sports, committee work, leader-
         ship, popular American hobbies.

IV.   Broad ethical, religious values, social
      responsibility.
         May take many forms, need not be
         active in religious group. May
         be grappling with concerns of
         tradition vs. modern problems,
         either by rebelling or by being
         active in church or synagogue.

"Finally, and above all, . . . "(same as
before except) "to promote good will" instead of "brotherhood."

47

Pages 3 through 5 of the research instrument present the candidates, each with the identical evaluation checklist at the bottom of the page. The candidates were prepared as follows:

Credentials for Candidates --

Three sets of credentials were drawn up in itemized style language with no reference to sex of candidate and no strongly sex-stereotyped activities listed. The credentials were then pretested on 72 male and female undergraduates who read the instructions and page 2 in standard English only, then ranked the credentials as to first, second and third choice, and finally indicated whether each set seemed appropriate for a male, female or either sex. Results demonstrated that each of the three credential sets were ranked first, second and third an approximately equal number of times. There was no tendency to assign "male" or "female" designations to any set of credentials, with the most common response being "either" (see Table 1).

TABLE 1

CREDENTIALS PRETEST FOR EQUIVALENCE

	1st Place	2nd Place	3rd Place	Male	Female	Either
Credentials Set 1	22 30.55%	22 31.94%	27 37.50%	11 15.27%	9 12.50%	50 72.22%
Credentials Set 2	26 35.11%	24 33.33%	22 30.55%	14 19.44%	15 20.83%	43 59.72%
Credentials Set 3	24 33.33%	25 34.72%	23 31.94%	9 12.50%	12 15.66%	51 70.83%

Despite this satisfactory pretest information, control procedures were still used to prevent any "credentials effect." The credentials were rotated in the acutal experiment and assigned alternately to the designation of male, female or unspecified. Assignment of sex was accomplished by use of a line atop the credentials stating:

> Basic information -- 18 years old, male (female or no sex term), good health and appearance.

Order effects were eliminated by thorough counterbalancing. Candidates were identified by "prison numbers" which were neutral with regard to preference connotations. Therefore, the procedures for preparing the candidates' credentials, assigning sex and ordering presentations were designed to minimize artifacts, obviousness and demand characteristics.

Ranking the Candidates and Personal Data

After reading about and scoring each candidate, the subjects proceeded to page 6 of the protocol, which consisted of the following items:

> "Now that you have studied and evaluated all three candidates, please place the number of each candidate on one appropriate space below:
>
> 1. _____ 2. _____ 3. _____
>   1st choice   2nd choice   3rd choice
>
> Please state the main reason for your preference.
>
> What do you think the objective of this study was?"

The rest of pages 6 through 8 asked for personal data with which to interpret the study, and opinion items which formed the Role Rigidity Scale (RRS) devised by me for the purposes of this research. The RRS was the last set of items in the protocol, after which it was written:

> "This concludes the study. If you have any questions, feel free to ask. Thank you very much for your help."

Papers were collected as they were finished, in order to assess whether in any group one language style or another tended to take respondents longer to finish. In particular, the non-sexist condition was held suspect, since the awkward-looking language could have hindered subjects. No such effect was observed in any of the groups and completed protocols were returned randomly with respect to treatment, just as they had been distributed.

Instruments

The participants in this study were asked to rank the three candidates, then to score them on a sex role instrument (Bem 1974) and then to give personal information about themselves, including the completion of the Caldie Role Rigidity Scale. The first instrument to be described is the Bem Sex Role Inventory.

Bem Sex Role Inventory: The bottom half of each candidate's credential page (pages 3, 4 and 5) contained the Bem Sex Role Inventory (1974), abbreviated BSRI:

> "This instrument was developed by having subjects select those adjectives which they associated with either male or females. A personality characteristic qualified as feminine if it was independently judged by both male and female judges to be significantly more desirable for a woman than for a man. The same process was undertaken for masculine characteristics."

Scores on the BSRI in the context of this study yield the degree to which each candidate was attributed with desirable masculine and desirable feminine traits by the subjects as a function of the independent variable or the subjects' organismic variables. Each candidate is given a masculinity and a femininity score by the subjects. The BSRI as reported by the originator, was first developed using two samples of undergraduates to select sex-appropriate adjectives and then these adjectives were scaled according to the degree to which they applied to some person. The BSRI has an internal consistency coefficient α = .86 for the masculinity scale, α = .81 for the femininity scale, and α = .75 for the social desirability response set. Test-retest reliability was at least r = .90. Validity measures are not available from Bem since this information was specifically designed to measure masculinity and femininity independent of each other, along with androgeny, which makes it unique, and according to Bem, incomparable to other instruments.

Nevertheless, in another pretest involving 34 undergraduate subjects, male and female, I had each candidate scored on both the BSRI and the Rosenkrantz, (1968) Sex Role Stereotype Scale as a partial indicator of construct validity. Pearson product moment correlation coefficients were r = .87, p $<$ .01 for the BSRI masculinity and the Rosenkrantz, and r = .85, p $<$ .01 for the BSRI femininity and the Rosenkrantz, indicating that the Bem was certainly tapping similar attributes to the more established Rosenkrantz.

The BSRI consists of sixty items (see Table 2) each with a 7-point Likert scale ranging from very like to very unlike the person being evaluated. From the following list of items, the only adaptation for this study involved item 56, the word "children" being changed to "people."

TABLE 2

Sandra L. Bem

ITEMS ON THE MASCULINITY, FEMININITY AND
SOCIAL DESIRABILITY SCALES OF THE BSRI

Masculine items		Feminine items		Neutral items	
49.	Acts as a leader	11.	Affectionate	51.	Adaptable
46.	Aggressive	5.	Cheerful	36.	Conceited
58.	Ambitious	50.	Childlike	9.	Conscientious
22.	Analytical	32.	Compassionate	60.	Conventional
13.	Assertive	53.	Does not use	45.	Friendly
10.	Athletic		harsh language	15.	Happy
55.	Competitive	35.	Eager to soothe	3.	Helpful
4.	Defends own		hurt feelings	48.	Inefficient
	beliefs	20.	Feminine	24.	Jealous
37.	Dominant	14.	Flatterable	39.	Likable
19.	Forceful	59.	Gentle	6.	Moody
25.	Has leadership	47.	Gullible	21.	Reliable
	abilities	56.	Loves children	30.	Secretive
7.	Independent	17.	Loyal	33.	Sincere
52.	Individualistic	26.	Sensitive to the	42.	Solemn
31.	Makes decisions		needs of others	57.	Tactful
	easily	8.	Shy	12.	Theatrical
40.	Masculine	38.	Soft spoken	27.	Truthful
1.	Self-reliant	23.	Sympathetic	18.	Unpredictable
34.	Self-sufficient	44.	Tender	54.	Unsystematic
16.	Strong personality	29.	Understanding		
43.	Willing to take	41.	Warm		
	a stand	2.	Yielding		
28.	Willing to take				
	risks				

Note: The number preceding each item reflects the position of each
       adjective as it actually appears on the Inventory.

Bem's adjective list is both comprehensive and subtle, developing an impression of the subjects' perception of the candidates. The goal of having BSRI scores for each candidate as well as ranks was to yield interpretations for any emergent treatment effects, to see if being preferred was related to being perceived as masculine, or if being discriminated against was associated with feminization.

In Bem's original work scoring focused on an androgeny concept, using the student's t-ratio between the total masculinity and total femininity tallies. In the present study, simple totals for the BSRI masculinity and femininity are separately recorded and analyzed for each candidate. The validity of Bem's t-ratio technique has been seriously challenged (Strahan 1975) on the grounds of violation of statistical assumptions, whereas sums and simple difference scores have been upheld. Though combined masculinity and femininity scales may yield an androgeny factor, such a new and relatively uninterpretable construct would lend little insight to the dependent variables in this study. Kept separate, masculinity and femininity scores could help isolate judgment factors operating in the assignment of ranks to candidates.

An additional instrument of value for interpreting this study was the subjects' level of role rigidity. Therefore, the second and last instrument to be described is the Caldie Role Rigidity Scale.

Caldie Role Rigidity Scale

Items on the Caldie Role Rigidity Scale (CRRS) were constructed to provide some data about the degree to which one's view on social flexibility account for sex preference of candidate. In other words, in order to interpret the dependent variables and to reduce confounding, it is important to cover all alternative or contributing explanations to language style (the treatment). The CRRS attempts to measure a type of social conservatism. This data contributes to external validity (generalizability) by carefully describing the sample, and to internal validity (effectiveness of treatment within the sample) by exploring competing interpretations of experimental effects (see Campbell and Stanley 1968).

In a pilot study, the CRRS was pretested for test-retest reliability on a sample of 32 college senior men and women at an interval of 10 days, for which $r = .93$. On another sample of 27 male and female undergraduates, $r = .86$ for a one-month interval between testings.

The Caldie Role Rigidity Scale contains ten items, each followed by a 5-point Likert scale ranging from strongly disagree to strongly agree. The items are:

1. Women should stay out of politics.

2. People can't be trusted.

3. The husband ought to have the say in family matters.

4. If a child is unusual in any way, the parents should try to make the child more like other children.

5. It is unnatural to place women in positions of authority over men.

6. Women need to worry about their appearance more than men do.

7. A wife cannot give as much to her career as a husband because she is usually more involved in family affairs than he is.

8. Male teenagers should not be expected to baby-sit.

9. If a child is allowed to talk back to the parents, there will be less respect in the family.

10. A wife's work should not interfere with her husband's career.

Subjects' total scores were taken as indicators of their degree of role rigidity, low scores indicating much flexibility. Although other related instruments could be found in the research literature (e.g., Spence & Helmreich's Attitude Toward Women Scale, 1972; Schmidt, 1974; Wortzel, et al., 1974 and Levinson and Hoffman's Traditional Family Ideology Scale, 1973) all the existing scales were either far too lengthy to administer with the protocol, excessively blunt about Women's Liberation, or obviously old-fashioned. Also, most had no available reliability or validity coefficients, making them no more desirable methodologically than the one compiled for this study. However, since the creation of the CRRS, I discovered that Halas (1974), Goldberg (1975), and Turner (1975) have all devised related instruments which may be of value in extensions of this study or in related research areas.

Although the CRRS is lacking validity coefficients, the outcomes of this study will yield data about the degree to which this scale can differentiate between members of the Kiwanis Club and NOW, between college aged youth and middle-aged adults. These data should establish a range of construct validity for the CRRS. Since the 10 CRRS items were derived from careful study of and analogizing from accepted items on scales of dogmatism (Lane 1955), authoritarianism (Rehfisch 1958), and role conceptualization (Wrightsman 1964), [16] the CRRS can be expected to vary significantly along educational, age-related and socioeconomic dimensions.

Thus, the instruments used in this study were selected to provide data on the detailed sex-role stereotyping to which the candidates have been exposed and the role conceptualization styles of the subjects doing the evaluating. Both of these areas of information will help to explain the ranking behaviors as the treatments operate upon the six groups of participants.

To summarize, the task for subjects in this experiment was to judge and to rank three candidates for an honorary position. Subjects were aware that this was a study concerning how such judgments and rankings are established, but hopefully the experimentor's interest in sex of the preferred candidate would not be obvious. The question asking the subject to state the purpose of the study, and the debriefing both must demonstrate the subject's desirable level of naivete. The assumption underlying this experiment is that since each candidate's credentials are closely equivalent in appeal, as documented by the pretests, the subjects should be scrutinizing the credentials quite closely for some discriminative qualities; sex of candidate is more likely to be salient under these conditions than when many other factors differentiate among the qualifications, thereby evoking sex biases.

If either the standard or non-sexist language styles of description are associated with preferences for a particular sex candidate, in contrast with the itemized control condition, then language may be implicated in forming attitudes toward the sexes. Randomization in assigning subjects to treatments, and specific testing of competing hypotheses helps to eliminate alternative explanations. The fact that sets of credentials are assigned on a rotation basis to the male, female and undesignated sexes represents an attempt to control for a credentials effect.[17] If the treatment has no effect, then each candidate should be selected in an approximately equal percent of cases over the total sampple. Since, however, theory justifies the hypothesizing of certain effects, departures from equality are to be expected. Chapter 4, the analysis of the data, will apply the predictions set forth under the research questions to the empirical outcomes of the study, to determine the relationships between language styles, role rigidity, sex-stereotyping and reactions to change in the context of this experiment.

[15]Adapted from 1974 Danforth Foundation Fellow-
ship Nomination forms.

[16]All these instruments are available in Robinson
and Shaver's <u>Measurements of Social Psychological
Attitudes</u>, University of Michigan, 1973.

[17]Methodologically, the use of names instead of
"sex: male;" "sex: female;" or no mention of
sex, to indicate a sex factor has been frequently cited in the literature (Walster and
Clifford, 1973; Clifford and Looft, 1973; Rosen,
Benson and Jerdee, 1974) as a valid procedure.
Photographs have also been used, which seems to
be a far more contaminated method than bland names.
However, the method used in this study seems the
least confounded from a methodological standpoint, because for the unspecified condition it
was risky to assume a name that has no sex connotations.

Chapter 4:   Analysis of Data

The three main research questions along with
their associated empirical hypotheses are tested in
this Chapter using the data gathered according to
the experimental procedure and instruments described
in the preceding Chapter. The main statistical techniques employed were analyses of variance with a 3
x 6 x 3 design and multiple correlation. To present a basic description of the sample of participants, raw data broken down by groups is presented
in Appendix B.

For the analysis of variance, the independent
variables were groups of subjects and treatments.
Analyses were run using the three candidates' ranks
as the dependent variables, and again using the
three candidates' Bem Sex Role Inventory (BSRI)
scores as dependent variables.

The multiple correlation technique was undertaken to seek out potentially valuable covariates,
to compare strengths of associations among organismic variables, and to reveal the relative values
and usefulness of the information obtained in the
study. In addition to the independent variables
of treatment and groups, each subject provided personal data of a demographic nature, then responded
to each candidate's BSRI form, and finally ranked
each candidate giving the reason for their preferences. Thus, there were a total of nine dependent variables for use as criteria of sex bias:
male candidate's rank, BSRI masculinity score and
BSRI femininity score; female candidate's rank,
BSRI masculinity score and BSRI femininity score;
unspecified candidate's rank, BSRI masuclinity score
and BSRI femininity score.

In all major analyses, programs of the
Statistical Package for the Social Sciences, 1975
version, were used to run computations. The
results of these techniques for evaluating each
dependent variable used to test the empirical hypotheses are presented as follows:

1. Male Candidate's Rank

        The dependent variable of the rank given
to the male candidate by the subject was designed
to test all three research questions through various empirical hypotheses. Table 3 provides the
analysis of variance results, with the only significant effect being a groups effect.

TABLE 3

Analysis of Variance: Male Candidate's Rank
by Groups by Treatment

Source	df	MS	F	F
Treatment	2	0.352	0.609	0.999
Groups	5	2.971	2.971	0.001
Interaction	10	0.680	0.680	0.308
Error	198	0.578	0.578	

        The absence of a significant treatment effect
bears heavily upon the first research question asks
if the degree of male pronoun dominance in language
affects the way people bestow status on males and
females. The first empirical hypothesis associated with this research question is that standard
(male pronoun dominant) English will be associated
with pro-male bias. This means that a significant
treatment effect, followed by a study of simple
contrasts, should show the standard treatment level
contributing substantially to favorable ranking for
the male candidate.

        Since there was no significant treatment effect,
and no significant interaction, no contrasts were
carried out and no support can be inferred for
this initial hypothesis from the first dependent
variable.

        The next empirical hypothesis which can be
partially tested by the analysis in Table 3 is
that itemized English (the control condition) is
associated with no sex biases. To begin suppor-

ting this hypothesis, it is necessary to demonstrate that the itemized treatment level did not contribute significantly to any tendency to rank males favorably or unfavorably. The absence of any treatment or interaction effects on the male candidate's rank constitutes partial support that the itemized treatment did not induce any sex bias. If it can be subsequently demonstrated that itemized English has no effect on any other dependent variable, this hypothesis will not be disconfirmed.

The analysis of variance for the male candidate's rank was of central importance in the testing of the last research question in this study. This question concerned the way groups of people react to linguistic change, and the possibility that conservative people would backlash. Specifically, the treatment condition of non-sexist language is viewed as unusual and progressive. The first empirical hypothesis states that the Kiwanis group would demonstrate backlash by increasing their pro-male or anti-female bias under the non-sexist treatment condition. Because the analyses of variance yielded no treatment effects upon the male candidate's rank, there was no further computation to determine if the effect of non-sexist English upon Kiwanis tended to increase pro-male bias. However, Figure 1 clearly reveals that non-sexist and standard English are both associated with the identical rank for the male candidate in the Kiwanis group. Therefore, no backlash can be inferred.

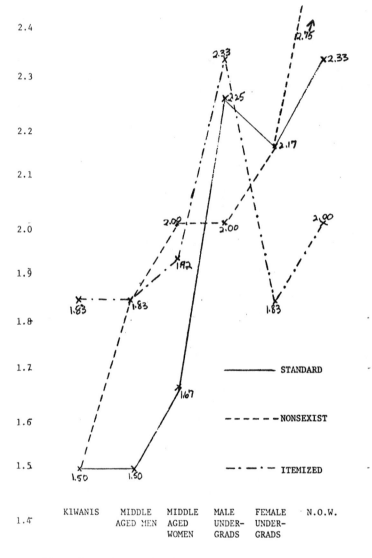

Figure 1 - Male Candidate's Mean Rank by Group and Treatment

The male candidate's rank was dependent variable in other analyses apart from the analysis of variance shown in Table 3. Correlational findings revealed associations that pertained to the relationship between role rigidity and sex bias. In consideration of the empirical hypothesis that role rigidity is directly related to pro-male bias, the correlation between rigidity scores and male rank ($r = -.30$ p $<$ .001) demonstrates that the more rigidity a subject displays, the better rank the subject gives to the candidate (i.e., the greater the pro-male bias). Low CRRS scores indicate high flexibility. There is a weak supporting association between rigidity and the female candidate's masculinity BSRI score ($r = .15$, p $<$ .025) and rigidity and the female candidate's BSRI score ($r = .14$, p $<$ .039), both indicating tendencies toward traditional stereotyping in people with high rigidity scores. However, the correlations between rigidity and the female's rank ($r = .113$, p $<$ .095) and rigidity and the male's BSRI score ($r = .085$, p $<$ .21 and $r = .091$, p $<$ .179) are not significant. Also, CRRS scores were not significantly correlated with any of the unspecified candidate's ranks or BSRI scores; this finding suggests that the unspecified candidate was a valid control condition for testing the first hypothesis that rigidity was related to pro-male bias.

Group effects in the analysis of variance could also be interpreted as reflections of the relationship between role rigidity and pro-male bias. Therefore, in Table 3, where the dependent variable was tapping the status of the male candidate (vis-a-vis rank), Table 3 documents a significant group effect on the male candidate's rank, which may result from group related differences in rigidity. (See Table 3, p. 58.)

Rigidity as a construct can be developed by considering some other correlational data from this study which are presented in Table 4.

TABLE 4

Variables Which Were Significantly Correlated
with Subject's Role Rigidity Scale Scores

Variable	Correlation Coefficient	P
Age of subject	.28	<.001
Sex of subject	.35	<.001
Education of subject	.19	<.005
Amount of religiosity of subject	.20	<.002
Male candidate's rank	-.30	<.001
Female candidate's BSRI masculinity score	.14	<.039

The associations between rigidity scores and characteristics such as age and sex impart an aspect of empirical validity to the construct of rigidity as a social psycholgical phenomenon. In fact, the six groups of subjects can be interpreted as representing sex and age-related rigidity levels, as illustrated in Table 5.

TABLE 5

Role Rigidity Scale Scores by Groups of Subjects

Group	Mean	Standard Deviation
Males		
Kiwanis	29.75	7.84
Middle-aged	27.90	8.02
Undergraduates	26.38	7.16
Females		
Middle-aged	26.39	5.32
Undergraduates	21.80	7.08
N.O.W.	18.55	7.10

The information in Table 5 provides a basis for interpreting any group effects in the analysis of variance as reflecting to some degree differences in role rigidity. This inference is based both upon the strong association between group membership and rigidity based upon theory and upon observed differences in group mean CRRS scores reported in Table 5. With this in mind, the significant group effect illustrated in Table 3 seems to support the hypothesis that high rigidity is related to pro-male bias.

The final hypothesis involving the male candidate's rank states that there will be a positive correlation between the age of the subject and the tendency to backlash. Inspection of Figure 1 reveals that best ranks for males under non-sexist treatment do not adhere to any fixed group-age-related patterns. Correlational data do not demonstrate significant negative correlation between age and male candidate's rank that would substantiate a claim of backlashing. A positive correlation between age and female candidate's rank which would also indicate backlashing as an enhanced anti-female bias, does not reach significance.

2. Male Candidate's BSRI Masculinity Score

The purpose of including the masculinity and femininity BSRI scores of each candidate was to be able to explain any treatment or groups effects upon ranks in terms of more detailed stereotyping trends. A low BSRI value indicates that the candidate has been attributed many characteristics generally associated with maleness in our culture. Table 6 displays the finding that no significant effects emerged using the male candidate's BSRI masculinity score as a criterion of sex stereotyping bias.

65

TABLE 6

Analysis of Variance: Male Candidate's BSRI
Masculinity Score by Groups by Treatment

Source	df	MS	F	P
Treatment	2	401.463	1.816	0.163
Groups	5	319.540	1.445	0.209
Interaction	10	178.152	0.806	0.999
Error	198	221.113		

These results bear upon the first two research
hypotheses in the exact same manner as the results
using the male candidate's rank as dependent variable:

    (1)   no support for the hypothesis that
            standard English is associated with
            pro-male bias,

    (2)   more partial support that itemized
            English is associated with no sex
            biases.

The hypothesis that role rigidity is directly
related to pro-male bias is not substaniated by
the male's BSRI masculinity score as it was by the
male's rank. As mentioned, the correlation between role rigidity and male's BSRI masculinity
score was only $r = .085$, $p < .21$.

The final set of "backlash" hypotheses were
not supported by the data in Table 6 as they partially were by the data in Table 3 using male's
rank. Therefore, it could not be substantiated
using male's BSRI masculinity scores in analysis
of variance or correlations that Kiwanis were backlashing or that older subjects tend to backlash.

3.   Male Candidate's BSRI Femininity Score

The BSRI femininity score indicates the degree
to which the candidate possesses characteristics
generally attributed to females in our society.
Low values indicate high femininity, just as low

BSRI masculinity scores indicate high masculinity.
The analysis of variance on the male candidate's
BSRI femininity scores summarized in Table 7 show
no significant effects, yet there is a trend toward
significance which could indicate that perhaps this
is more evidence of how our culture is more sensitive to males' deviant femininity than they are to
males' attainment of normal masculinity.

TABLE 7

Analysis of Variance: Male Candidiate's BSRI
Femininity Score by Groups by Treatment

Source	df	MS	F	P
Treament	2	444.500	2.866	0.060
Groups	5	323.511	2.086	0.070
Interaction	10	109.578	0.707	0.999
Error	198	155.080		

Although Table 7 shows F values approaching significance, the dependent variable is not significantly correlated with treatment, groups, role rigidity or any other major variable in the study,
thereby reducing the potential importance of this
trend. Therefore, accepting the nonsignificance
or borderline status of the scores, Table 7 results relate to the hypotheses exactly as Table 6
did.

4. Female Candidate's Rank

     The next set of dependent variables relates to
the status attributed to the female candidate.
This information is necessary to evaluate the hypothesis that non-sexist language would be associated
with pro-female bias. Operationally this means a
treatment effect should emerge on the following
dependent variables: (1) female candidate's rank;
(2) female candidate's BSRI masculinity score; and
(3) female candidate's BSRI femininity score.
These scores should indicate preferences for fe-

67

males and absence of adverse sex stereotyping.
Table 8 shows the analysis of variance summary
table for the female candidate's rank, demonstrating no empirical support from this study for the
hypothesis that non-sexist language induces a pro-
female bias.

TABLE 8

Analysis of Variance: Female's Rank
by Groups by Treatment

Source	df	MS	F	P
Treatment	2	0.130	0.223	0.999
Groups	5	2.785	4.782	0.001
Interaction	10	0.330	0.566	0.999
Error	198	0.582		

Turning to the next hypothesis, that itemized
English induces no biases, the absence of any treatment effect on the female's rank adds more support
to the previously-mentioned results. First it was
shown in Tables 3, 6 and 7 that the itemized treatment did not affect the male candidate's dependent
variables and here it is shown that the female's
rank is unaffected as well.

Table 8 does, however, display a significant
group effect which bears upon the hypotheses associated with the second research question. This
question generally addresses the relationship between role rigidity and sex biases. The actual
empirical hypothesis states that high rigidity is
associated with pro-male bias, but as an alternative indicator, anti-female bias can be associated
with high rigidity or pro-female bias can be
associated with low rigidity. Therefore, the data
in Table 8 can be taken as evidence supporting the
specific contention that N.O.W., the group with
the lowest CRRS mean score, would display significant pro-female biases across all treatment conditions. The significant group effect was the

basis for carrying out a series of contrasts in the
next step of analysis.

The next step of analysis involved demonstrating that the N.O.W. group's scores were contributing to the observed group effect, and that the
female candidate's rank as the criterion (Table 8),
the group means arranged in order of decreasing
preference are:

1.53	1.67	1.98	2.03	2.09	2.28
Male	N.O.W.	Female	Female	Male	Kiwanis
Under-		Under-	Middle-	Middle-	
graduates		graduates	Aged	Aged	

Using the Newman-Keuls computation for simple
contrasts at the .05 level of significance, N.O.W.
and the other groups did not perform significantly
differently from each other, except that N.O.W.'s
ranking of the female was significantly lower than
that of the Kiwanis group. However, male undergraduates displayed at least as great a pro-female
bias as did N.O.W. to the extent that the male
undergraduate's mean rank was significantly lower
than all other groups except N.O.W. To explore
whether the low female rank given by the N.O.W.
group exists across all three treatment conditions,
a breakdown of female's rank by treatment by groups
was done, and Figure 2 illustrates the results in
profile form:

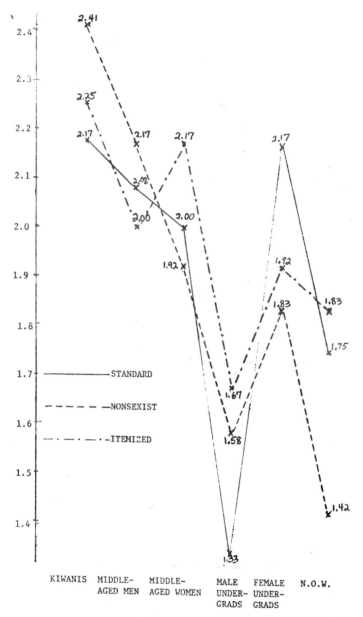

Figure 2 - Female Candidate's Mean Rank by Group and Treatment

70

Analysis of these N.O.W. mean scores using the
Newman-Keuls test indicated the mean for the non-
sexist treatment is significantly different from
both the itemized and standard conditions, and
that the latter two treatment levels are not significantly different from each other. Since within
the N.O.W. group there are significant differences
among treatment means, pro-female bias is enhanced
under non-sexist language conditions. However,
Figure 2 clearly illustrates that N.O.W. was not
the most pro-female group, N.O.W. being surpassed
by the male undergraduates. Therefore, since
treatment did show some effect and another group
actually ranked females more preferentially, this
research hypothesis is only partially supported.
N.O.W. does display significant pro-female biases,
but not across all treatment conditions and not as
pro-female as the male undergraduates.

The next hypothesis for which the female candidate's rank is a criterion is that other organismic variables of the subject will moderate the
effect of the experimental treatment (language
style) on the various criteria of sex bias operating through the intervening variable of role conceptualization. A modification of this hypothesis
must be made before any analysis can be of value:
Other organismic variables of the subject are
related to the various criteria of sex bias, but
they do not necessarily operate by moderating the
effect of the experimental treatment, since it will
be demonstrated that there was no major treatment
effect in the entire study. Treatment had only a
small effect on one dependent variable, the unspecified candidate's BSRI masculinity score. The
other organismic variable which was related to the
female candidate's rank was age ($r = .19$, $p < .005$).

The group effect documented in Table 8 and
illustrated in Figure 2 supports another empirical
hypothesis, that Kiwanis will backlash under the
non-sexist treatment condition. The female candidate's ranks charted in Figure 1 reveal a nonsigni-
ficant trend toward a backlash effect because under
the non-sexist English condition the female was

ranked less favorably than in any other treatment or for any other group. This tendency also appears for middle-aged men, bearing upon the following final hypothesis.

The final hypothesis relating age of the subject to tendency to backlash is not confirmed by either analysis of variance or correlation, but Figure 2 graphically suggests that groups with greatest mean age scores (see Appendix B) rank the female least preferentially.

Summing up the data on female's rank, the surprising finding that the male undergraduates showed the greatest pro-female bias and the expected finding that middle-aged men and Kiwanis evaluated the female least favorably both come from the observed group effect in Table 8. The next dependent variable, female candidate's BSRI masculinity score, was intended to clarify the above findings.

5. Female Candidate's BSRI Masculinity Score

The BSRI masculinity score for the female candidate indicates the extent to which subjects attributed her with characteristics customarily associated with males in our culture. This variable was intended to help provide interpretations for treatment effects appearing on the main dependent variables, which were the ranks. As Table 9 shows, neither the treatments nor the groups had any statistically significant effect upon the female candidate's BSRI masculinity score.

TABLE 9

Analysis of Variance: Female's BSRI
Masculinity Score by Groups by Treatment

Treatment	2	282.889	1.691	0.185
Groups	5	206.631	1.235	0.293
Interaction	10	1.910	1.910	0.045
Error	198			

72

These main effects results, since they do not reach statistical significance, cannot be employed to explain the group effect on the male rank or the trend toward significance of both group and treatment effects in the male candidate's BSRI femininity score. The significant interaction which does appear does not relate to any of the hypotheses being tested in this study. However, the final dependent variable does contain a significant main effect of interest.

6.   Female Candidate's BSRI Femininity Score

The purpose of this dependent variable was to ascertain the degree to which the subject attributed characteristics customarily associated with females in our culture to the female candidate. Then, the results of analyses on female candidate's rank could be interpreted.

Table 10 provides the statistical results which document a significant group effect on the female candidate's BSRI femininity score.

TABLE 10

Analysis of Variance: Female's BSRI
Femininity Score by Groups by Treatment

Source	df	MS	F	P
Treatment	2	267.032	1.427	0.241
Groups	5	1060.303	5.666	0.001
Interaction	10	202.170	1.080	0.379
Error	198	187.128		

This group effect is directly relevant to the hypotheses that (1) N.O.W. will display pro-female bias across all treatment conditions, and (2) Kiwanis would backlash under the condition of non-sexist English. The first hypothesis requires that the N.O.W. mean score be significantly different from every other group in all three treatment levels.

The female candidate's BSRI mean scores for each group are presented in order of decreasing femininity:

58.78	64.14	64.33	67.92	72.61	72.69
Male Under- graduates	Female Under- graduates	N.O.W.	Middle- Aged Men	Middle- Aged Women	Kiwanis

Newman-Keuls contrasts at the .05 level of significance show that the N.O.W. group is signi- ficantly different from only the Kiwanis Club mem- bers and middle-aged women, and N.O.W. affiliates did not score the female candidate significantly differently from any of the other groups. Moreover, the N.O.W. treatment means which should not be significantly different from each other for this hypothesis to be supported, can be analyzed by Newman-Keuls contrasts after arranging the means in order of decreasing femininity:

59.75	61.33	71.92
non-sexist	standard	itemized

Standard and itemized treatments are signifi- cantly different from each other, and itemized and non-sexist are significantly different from each other, but non-sexist and standard conditions do not have significantly different means. Therefore, it seems that for N.O.W., treatment may have an effect, rendering this hypothesis unsupported by the data.

The hypothesis involving Kiwanis backlashing can be evaluated by a set of group means analogous to those used to analyze the preceding hypothesis. For it to be substantiated that Kiwanis are back- lashing, their mean score should be significantly different from all the other groups, in a direction indicating anti-female bias, under the non-sexist treatment level. The non-sexist treatment level group means follow:

74

74.41	70.4167	69.33	69.17	59.75	55.33
Kiwanis	Middle-Aged Women	Female Under-graduates	Middle-Aged Men	N.O.W.	Male Under-graduates

Kiwanis scored significantly differently from male undergraduates and N.O.W., but not from all other groups; therefore, it cannot be argued that Kiwanis are backlashing, especially since it seems that it is the N.O.W. and male undergraduate factions who are deviating in an ultra-pro-female direction rather than the Kiwanis who are reactionary, and ultra-pro-female relative to the six groups in this study.

Turning to the final set of dependent variables, involving the unspecified candidate's rank and BSRI scores, the rank will be the first variable to be considered.

7. Unspecified Candidate's Rank

The unspecified candidate's criteria were included in the set of dependent variables as a control condition and to eliminate a forced choice between male and female candidates by providing an alternative. Since there would then be three candidates to rank, the range of rank scores would increase, enhancing the potential for analysis of the data.

Table 11 presents the unspecified candidate's rank by group by treatment analysis of variance. There were no significant effects at all, indicating that no extraneous factors were operating beyond those accounted for in the experimental design according to these data. Figure 3, also illustrating a breakdown of treatment and group means, further demonstrates no significant trends in the data.

TABLE 11

Analysis of Variance: Unspecified Candidate's
Rank by Groups by Treatment

Source	df	MS	F	F
Treatment	2	0.296	0.395	0.999
Groups	5	0.527	0.702	0.999
Interaction	10	0.674	0.898	0.999
Error	198	0.750		

76

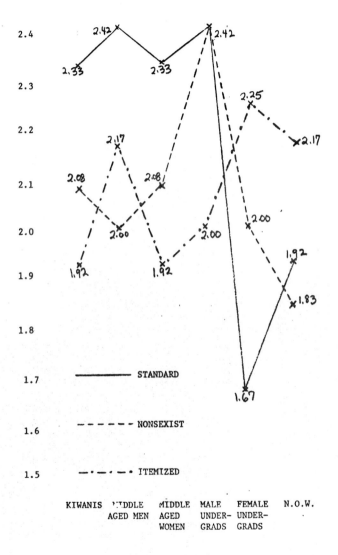

Figure 3 - Unspecified Candidate's Mean Rank by Group and Treatment

77

8. Unspecified Candidate's BSRI Masculinity Score

Table 12 summarizes the analysis of variance results on the unspecified candidate's BSRI masculinity score. Results relate to the third empirical hypothesis associated with the first research question, that itemized English (the control condition) should be associated with no sex biases. This prediction operationally states that no effect should ever emerge involving the treatment condition of itemized English, and indeed, none ever does on any dependent variables. Tables 3 and 6 through 10 have already documented no significant treatment effects for all dependent variables associated with the male and female candidates, and the following Table 12 presents the analyses of variance involving the unspecified candidate's BSRI masculinity score where effects do emerge:

TABLE 12

Analysis of Variance: Unspecified Candidate's BSRI Masculinity Score by Groups by Treatment

Source	df	MS	F	P
Treatment	2	1142.055	4.125	0.017
Groups	5	226.253	0.817	0.999
Interaction	10	600.496	2.169	0.021
Error	198	276.890		

The observed treatment effect must be accounted for by the standard and non-sexist treatment conditions, and not by the itemized level, to support this hypothesis, since the hypothesis states that itemized English should result in no sex biases.

Newman-Keuls contrasts carried out on the unspecified candidate's treatment mean masculinity BSRI scores yielded the following results:

47.41	52.68	55.21
standard	itemized	non-sexist

The standard and non-sexist conditions are significantly different from each other but neither is
significantly different from the itemized condition. Therefore, the itemized English does not
appear to be associated with sex biases even in
the one instance where treatment effects emerged.
Itemized English, a sex neutral treatment level,
would be associated with sex biases only if such
biases existed independent of linguistic considerations; that is, if attitudes account for biases
without any effect of sexism in language. No such
biases appeared in this data.

9. Unspecified Candidate's BSRI Femininity Score

        The final dependent variable analyzed in
Table 13 shows no significant effects and contributes to the overall validity of the experimental
design and procedure.

TABLE 13

Analysis of Variance: Unspecified Candidate's
BSRI Femininity Score by Groups by Treatment

Treatment	2	341.911	1.534	0.217
Groups	5	241.260	1.082	0.372
Interaction	10	115.928	0.520	0.999
Error	198	222.959		

It appears that the unspecified candidate and
itemized English are both free of association with
any significant experimental effects.

        From consideration of the unspecified candi-
date's dependent variables, it seems a promising
possibility that removal of sex identification from
materials such as job applications may effectively

reduce discrimination, probably more effectively
than eliminating male pronoun dominance from the
job description.

Summary

    Summarizing the analysis of data from the van-
tage point of the hypotheses rather than dependent
variables:

1. Standard English will be associated with pro-
    male biases, not supported;

2. Non-sexist English will be associated with
    pro-female bias, not supported;

3. Itemized English will not be associated with
    any sex bias, supported;

4. The greater the Role Rigidity Scale score of
    the subject, the stronger the pro-male bias
    (or the greater the anti-female bias),
    supported;

5. Other demograghic variables of the subject
    will moderate or supplant the effect of the
    treatment on the various criteria of sex bias,
    operating through the intervening variable
    of role conceptualization, supported;

6. Subjects drawn from a population of N.O.W.
    affiliates would display pro-female biases
    across all treatment conditions, partially
    supported;

7. Subjects drawn from a population of Kiwanis
    Club members will show a backlash effect
    under the non-sexist language treatment con-
    dition (manifested by enhanced pro-male or
    anti-female biases), weak trend toward support;

8. There will be a positive correlation between
    the age of the subject and the tendency to
    backlash, not supported.

    The conclusions based on these findings along
with limitations and implications of this research
will be discussed in the next Chapter.

Chapter 5:   Summary, Conclusions and
              Directions for Further Research

SUMMARY:

In this experimental study, six groups of subjects were given descriptions of an honorary position for which they were to rank three candidates.
The description was written either in standard, non-
sexist or itemized English. The three candidates
were one female, one male and one unspecified person. Along with ranks, participants gave each candidate an evaluation on the Bem Sex Role Inventory
and provided information about their own back-
grounds.

Before presenting details of the procedure,
instruments and analysis, a review of the literature was presented which explored three main research questions, each with associated empirical
hypotheses and a basic theoretical issue.

The first theoretical issue dealt with the
form and content of language as factors which develop and maintain sex roles and biases. It was
hypothesized that (1) standard English would be
associated with pro-male bias, (2) non-sexist
English would be associated with pro-female bias,
and (3) itemized English would not be associated
with any sex bias. The literature review established a lengthy history of male dominance in
both the form and content of language, and a
parallel male dominance in achievement and self-
esteem. Through the standard use of a masculine
generic, an overrepresentation of male protago-
nists (at least 6:1), a persistent inferior
characterization of females, and male-dominated
word order, the theory was developed that language serves as a socializing force which helps
to form and to maintain sex roles and biases.

Mechanisms by which language may operate as a
socializing force were explained, primarily invol-

ving an associative conditioning paradigm which
inhibits achievement in females and facilitates
active performance in males. Both semantic and
syntactic levels contribute to the existence of
communication codes that separate the sexes. Even
at levels of phonemes and morphemes, as well as at
more complex linguistic levels, males and females
generate and interpret language differently. Evidence for these assertions provides a basis for
the argument that male and female language styles
are self-perpetuating systems which socialize each
new child as language is acquired, along those
dimensions wherein communication styles of the
sexes differ. Hence, the treatment condition of
standard English should interrupt the traditional
pro-male bias, non-sexist English should interrupt
the traditional pattern, and the itemized condition should be associated with only those biases
which are not related to language.

The second theoretical issue involved an alternative to the previous view of the relationship
between language and culture. Rather than language
shaping culture, this view states that our attitudes (in this case, role conceptualizations)
influence or even determine language. Therefore,
by this view, language is more a reflection of
society than a socializing force. Language takes
on the attributes of a people-constructed tool,
meaning that people have considerable control over
both the production and interpretation of language,
in line with their ideas about reality. The hypotheses that were tested in connection with this
theory were that (1) Caldie Role Rigidity Scale
scores would be directly related to pro-male bias
(in lieu of language as the determining factor),
(2) other subject variables will influence the
treatment effect, or in modified form, supplant the
treatment effect, and (3) the sample of N.O.W.
affiliates would display consistent pro-female
biases across all treatment conditions. The last
hypothesis is based on the assumption that N.O.W.
represents a population whose sex bias attitudes
are at the far liberal end of the spectrum. Such

extreme attitudes are the most likely to influence or to override the short-term effects of language.

The literature review around this second question focused upon roles and attitudes as providing the most salient social contexts in which people as psychological "actors" choose and manipulate language to serve their purposes. Bernstein's (1961, 1964) elaborated and restricted codes and person and object modes were offered as examples of linguistic styles which reflect differing socially determined needs and capacities of individuals from, expression. A pattern wherein role innovation generally precedes language reform was established, and the converse, where role expectancies drastically limit progressive or innovative language behavior particularly along sex-appropriate lines, was documented. Both patterns view language as an effect more than a cause. Therefore, the literature offered considerable evidence that language reflects one's socialization history rather than accounting for it.

The trend of behavioral science research, as it tests basic theories of causes and effects, has been first to test one factor as a cause for another, then to evaluate the alternative, that what was formerly viewed as the effect may indeed be a significant cause; finally, interaction is suggested, wherein both factors in a system of dynamic equilibrium continuously influence each other. The first two research questions with their associated empirical hypotheses and theoretical issues follow this traditional pattern.

The third and final research question, dealing with the problem of linguistic change, does not concern itself with causality. It simply attempts to examine from a practical, applied standpoint how people will react when language reform is imposed by unnatural means. Change and causality pose insurmountable problems in the philosophy of science, and are considered in this review only insofar as imposed language change may impede or facilitiate sex-role stereotyping behavior, and not as a study of the phenomenon of change per se in any social-psychological context.

Specifically, it was hypothesized that (1) non-sexist language would be associated with a backlash effect in Kiwanis Club subjects, and (2) older subjects in general would also tend to backlash. Kiwanis are known as social traditionalists who uphold conservative values. They also represent a professional population who would possibly feel threatened by increasing opportunities and status for females. Since their official policy explicitly (and as recently as February 1981) excludes women from their organization, they have certainly considered the current status of women and opted against equality of the sexes.

A reactionary response to the non-sexist treatment condition was hypothesized as a result of observing popular reactions to feminist language reforms. Early conservative outrage directed at the terms "Ms." and "chairperson" was vigorous enough to suggest a defensive or at least self-interested overtone. Males and females alike, who were vocal critics, stressed the "natural order" and the needs of society in maintaining the linguistic status quo. The review of the literature explores change in language usage as being most effective if the change is socially significant and embodies desirable interpersonal consequences for the language user. Therefore, to those threatened by equality of the sexes, language reform must be resisted, change must be suppressed in the hope that contingent social consequences can be avoided or minmized.

The particular language change in this experiment is in the written mode, and accurately represents the offical changes being instituted by publication, organizational and governmental guidelines. Yet natural processes of language change begin in the spoken mode and take years of popularization before they are assimilated into the formal written mode. This reversal of the natural process of change may invite backlashing on the part

of traditionally reactionary groups who might have
accepted the changes had they been more gradual
and preceded by spoken reforms. Therefore, groups
of subjects were chosen to represent populations
who would be expected to respond differently from
each other to the three styles of language used in
the experimental treatment.

Groups of Subjects

In the design of this study, subject variables
which seemed most likely to influence reactions to
language change were age, sex and some dimension
of social conservatism. Groups of subjects were
selected to represent youth and middle-aged males
and females, and two opposite extremes in social
conservatism, Kiwanis who have no feminist or
liberal associations, and affiliates of the National
Organiztion for Women (N.O.W.) who have an extremely
feminist orientation, with strong liberal associations.

The male and female youth were college undergraduates, mostly freshmen and sophomores in intro-
ductory English courses at a large Cleveland area
university. The middle-aged males and females were
members of various community social groups, mostly
church-affiliated with one hospital volunteer group
included. Two Cleveland area Kiwanis Clubs and
three N.O.W. chapters provided participants to
represent those populations. Each group of subjects is described in Appendix B in terms of the
means and standard deviations of all non-nominal
personal data obtained in this study.

Procedure

The experimental procedure involved distribu-
ting the research instrument to the groups of subjects during one of their normal meetings. Cover
instructions were read aloud. Within each group,
subjects randomly received only one of the three

language styles (treatment level) and all respondents took approximately twenty-five minutes to complete the protocol. Responses were collected and subjects were told the entire purpose and design of the study. Subjects' reactions and input provided important information with which to interpret their responses.

Following analysis of the data, results were offered to all the cooperating groups, Individual anonymity was guaranteed, and only group effects were discussed.

Findings

To facilitate a discussion of the findings, a summary of the empirical hypotheses is offered:

1. Standard English will be associated with pro-male bias.

2. Non-sexist English will be associated with pro-female bias.

3. Itemized English will not be associated with any sex bias.

4. The greater the Caldie Role Rigidity Scale score of the subject, the stronger the pro-male bias (or the greater the anti-female bias).

5. Other demographic variables of the subject will moderate or supplant the effect of the treatment on the various criteria of sex bias, operating through the intervening varible of role conceptualization.

6. Subjects drawn from a population of N.O.W. affiliates would display pro-female biases across all treatment conditions.

7. Subjects drawn from a population of Kiwanis

Club members will show a backlash effect
under the non-sexist language treatment
condition (manifested by enhanced pro-male
or anti-female biases).

8.   There will be a positive correlation between
the age of the subject and tendancy to backlash.

Regarding the first hypothesis, the data did
not demonstrate any significant assocation between
standard English and pro-male bias using the dependent variables of male rank or male BSRI scores.
Analysis of variance yielded no significant treatment effects.

Similarly, the second hypothesis also lacked
empirical support. The analysis of variance yielded
no significant treatment effects upon the dependent
variables of female candidate's rank or BSRI scores,
and no association between the non-sexist treatment and pro-female bias could be inferred.

The third hypothesis did receive support from
this study. Itemized English was not associated
with any effects on any dependent variables. In
the one significant treatment effect wherein the
unspecified candidate's masculinity BSRI score was
affected by the treatment, the itemized condition
was not contributing to the effect.

The fourth hypothesis which posits a direct
relationship between Caldie Role Rigidity Scale
scores and pro-male bias is supported by a correlation of $r = -.30$, $p < .001$ between RRS scores
and the male candidate's rank. Additionally,
significant group effects upon the male candidate's
rank in the analysis of variance show high rigidity
groups giving male much better ranks than low
rigidity groups. Alternatively, there is a slight
tendency for low rigidity groups to rank the female candidate more preferably than do high rigidity groups.

Other subject variables which moderate or supplant the treatment effect are the domain of the fifth hypothesis in this study. Those variables should form a construct tapping the subject's role conceptualizations. The rigidity variable is the basic indicator of social attitudes, but the data indicate that age, sex, education and religion are correlated both with rigidity and with the dependent variables indicative of sex bias. This fifth hypothesis, that other variables besides rigidity and the treatment affect the dependent variables, tends to be supported. In the absence of any strong treatment effect, it stands to reason that other factors besides the experimental manipulation have influenced the outcome. However, had there been a pronounced treatment effect, then this hypothesis may well have been disconfirmed.

The sixth hypothesis, that N.O.W. affiliates would be consistenly pro-female across all treatment conditions, was partially supported by the data. N.O.W. proved consistently and significantly more pro-female than the Kiwanis, but not significantly more so than any of the other groups. Also, male undergraduates were even more pro-female than N.O.W. Finally, the N.O.W. pro-female performance was significantly enhanced under the non-sexist treatment condition, meaning that the treatment did have some effect even though the group was already extremely biased.

Next, the seventh hypothesis deals with Kiwanis Club members backlashing under the non-sexist treatment condition. Although the objective of non-sexist language reform is to equalize opportunities for both sexes, or even to promote females, exactly the opposite result may occur in groups who are resistent to change in general, or hostile to aspiring females in particular. Non-sexist English may arouse these people's antagonism or insecurities, resulting in even greater pro-male bias at the expense of females. In support of this hypothesis, the female ranked least preferably in the non-sexist condition ($\bar{X}$ = 2.41) and most favorably in the standard condition ($\overline{X}$ = 2.17) by the Kiwanis, and no other groups except middle-aged men give the female such an undesirable rank in the non-sexist condition.

However, looking at the male candidate's ranks in Figure 2 (page 73), it is impossible to infer that Kiwanis are backlashing by increasing their pro-male bias in the non-sexist condition, because they give the identical mean rank score to the male candidate in both the standard and non-sexist treatments ($\overline{X}$ = 1.50). Thus, while the Kiwanis seem to be backlashing on the dependent variable of female candidate's ranks, they do not display this tendency when ranking the male. Such a tendency can be suspected when the male is ranked best in the non-sexist condition, which only happens in the male undergraduate group.

The final hypothesis, that a tendency to backlash and age are positively correlated, cannot be substantiated from the data on the male candidate's rank as was just demonstrated, but is suggested from the data on the female candidate. On this latter dependent variable, both Kiwanis and middle-aged men (the two oldest groups) ranked the female as considerably less desirable in the non-sexist condition. However, it must be restated here that throughout the data analysis, no significant treatment effect emerged on either the male or female candidate's dependent variables. Hence, the non-sexist condition cannot be assoicated with significantly different ranks for either the male or female candidate, and only tendencies can be noted.

CONCLUSIONS:

Interpretation of Findings

The results of this empirical research indicate that language as a tool for short-term attitude control (counteraction of sex biases) has little, if any, effect. The first two hypotheses, that standard English promotes pro-male bias, and non-sexist English promotes pro-female bias, are not adequately supported.

Language undoubtedly is a very salient socializing force, as the review of the literature indicates, yet the value of language in short-term resocialization is quite dubious in light of these data. Clearly, then, there must be important differences, both qualitative and quantitative between the experiences of socialization and resocialization. By the age level of the youngest subjects in this study (18 years old) major socialization experiences have occured and solidified. The most sensitive period to the weltanshaungs contained by language is past, and by now the person is a user of language, not a totally impressionable mind ready to be molded by language.

The interpretation of the findings wherein the third hypotheis is supported, is that neutral language (itemized treatment) does not reveal any attitudes of bias which exist independent of language. Either people sensitively monitor and suppress such biases when under the demand characteristics of the experiment, or such biases do not exist. The first possible explanation is contradicted by the subjects' responses to the questions "What do you think the purpose of this study was?" and "Why did you rank the candidates as you did?" Neither question revealed any awareness that sex biases were being studied. A few subjects in the N.O.W. group voiced objections to the standard English condition in the debriefing-discussion following the data collection. They began to mention issues of sexism spontaneously, but never expressed the opinion that this study was exploring sexisim or language in any way.

The second explanation, that biases do not exist, is also quite unlikely given the pro-male responses of the Kiwanis, the pro-female responses of N.O.W. and the surprising, even stronger pro-female responses of the male undergraduates. The groups effects which appeared in the absence of treatment effects must largely reflect group-related biases; however, itemized English does not elicit such differences and in this light may be a better social "remedy" than non-sexist English for the reduction of sexism in language.

The finding that male undergraduates displayed even stronger pro-female bias than N.O.W. is intriguing, and substantiates a trend proposed in the review of the literature by Yerby (1974) wherein young educated males undergo high rates of role change to adjust to more challenging, less passive females around them. By adopting and even surpassing their female peers' feminist attitudes, young college men can avoid the conflicts of interacting with women who threaten their alleged superiority.

The interpretation of the empirical support for the fourth hypothesis, that role rigidity is positively correlated with pro-male bias, is that the more rigid a person is, the more favoritism will be granted to men. Such a finding competes with the theory that the degree of male pronoun dominance in language will directly influence sex stereotyping behavior. Rigidity, already socialized into a person's set of attitudes, beliefs and norms, may have been a product of early, linguistically-encoded world views, but by college age becomes an autonomous factor influencing the relative ranks given to males and females. Merging with the fifth hypothesis, that other subject variables besides rigidity influence the dependent variables, it seems substantiated that characteristics which subjects bring to the experimental situation account for far more of the effect on the dependent variables than any of the treatments do.

The logical extension of the previous two hypotheses was the basis for this, the sixty hypothesis: Subjects drawn from a population of N.O.W. affiliates would display pro-female biases across all treatment conditions. In effect, this N.O.W. group would have such a strong predisposition that no treatment would have any influence on the dependent variables.

The lack of complete support for this hypothesis indicates that there is still room for social action attempts via language reform, but that the magnitude of the impact is likely to be inconsistent, unpredictable and disappointing.

The seventh hypothesis, also related to the socialization factors which influence people's receptivity or permeability to language reform, was that Kiwanis would backlash under non-sexist treatment. There was not adequate support for this hypothesis to substantiate backlash as the empirical conservative's reaction to imposed linguistic change. Throughout the analysis of data on each hypothesis, the subjects seem to be proactive, impervious to the attempted manipulation of their sex-role stereotyping behavior, and deliberate in their actual judgment of the candidates.

Similarly, in the final research hypothesis, the failure to substantiate strong relationships between age and tendency to backlash adds an extra element of autonomy to the subjects' performance.

Limitations

This study was designed to provide a review of theory and research, and current data on an immediately pressing issue of sexism in language. Dealing only with adults, there was no input as to the formative stages of language--culture relationships. Therefore, the emergent role of language in the formation of sex-role attitudes cannot be assessed.

A methodological limitation involving the possible effects of sex of experimentor should be mentioned. The experimentor was a 25-year old woman, a factor which may have induced some systematic biases, probably pro-female.

Another limitation of this study involves the
use of the Caldie Role Rigidity Scale which was
devised for the purpose of this study. As such,
the CRRS has not been validated extensively, and
can only be evaluated in light of the pretest data
provided the experimental outcomes of this study.

If the reality considerations of availability
of subjects, and amount of time required for subjects to complete the protocol were not as pressing
as they were, the limitations of incomplete samp-
ling of subjects and brevity of treatment could be
overcome. Other groups which could profitably be
studied would be adolescents, the aged and different racial and cultural minorities representing
particular sex role socialization patterns. Treatment could involve several related tasks and con-
sist of more than one page of orienting material.

In actual administration of the protocol, some
of the older subjects (approximately 10%) appeared
somewhat confused by the instruments used in the
study. Though the procedure for these people was
not altered, perhaps special instructions for
older subjects may be valuable to orient them on
an equal basis with those subjects already fami-
liar with Likert scales, repeated measures and
questionnaires in general.

Another limitation of this study was the absence of a fourth treatment condition--female pronoun dominant English. This treatment would have
yielded data on the effect of exclusive use of
female pronouns upon the dependent variables.

Finally, a limitation of the statistical analysis involved the local unavailability as yet of
certain computer programs which would have provided
valuable techniques for analyzing the data in this
study. Alternative techniques were undertaken,
and the ones of choice will be carried out pending
implementation of the desired subprograms in dis-
criminant analysis.

94

Implications

The results of this study suggest that language style, while having enormous social significance, does not control short-term sex-role stereotyping behavior as manifest by ranks and BSRI scores. Therefore, though the current efforts toward eliminating sexism in language may be valuable gestures of egalitarianism on the part of the language user, they cannot be assumed to have influence over the language receiver.

Indeed, it seems that itemized English is associated with less biases than either standard or non-sexist English; itemized English seems less "offensive" than non-sexist English to conservative groups and may be a preferable social "remedy" in situations where linguistic reform appears desirable. In any case, the findings of this study certainly can be used to recommend against any large allocation of resources for non-sexist language reform, since the overall effect is so negligible.

Apart from the practical implications, the experimental results have theoretical implications as well. The three theoretical issues were resolved as follows: (1) the form and content of language may develop and maintain sex roles in childhood, but by the stage of early adulthood, people do not display much responsiveness to short-term language manipulation; (2) our role conceptualizations (as functions of rigidity, sex, age and education) do indeed influence and often override the effects of language style; and (3) the unnatural patterns of language change imposed by current guidelines and legislation do not cause any large scale backlash effects or reactionary responses in a sample of conservative males. The unnatural non-sexist English may be awkward and ineffective as a sexual equilizer, it is not offensive and disruptive to any great degree.

Overall, as adults, it seems more likely that we control our use of language than that our language

usage controls our thoughts and attitudes. That
this is true of children as well as adults is most
difficult to contend, since the data are not available for children. This observation leads to the
final section of this study, entitled Recommendations
for Research.

RECOMMENDATIONS FOR RESEARCH:

A follow-up study with an analogous design and
simplified task should be run on the youngest possible groups of literate children. Then a verbal
adaptation of the task should be administered to
even younger children. There may be an age at
which the specific sex dominance used in the orientation will influence sex preferences of candidates.
This may mark the transition point in the interre-
lationship between culture and language.

A search for a more extensively validated role
rigidity measure should be made among the very
recently devised instruments in the event that a
better measure is now available for·use in follow-
up studies.

Another treatment level of female pronoun dominant language should be run to document empirically
the effect which exclusive use of "she" and "her"
has on the dependent variables. Contrasting groups
of different ethnic, economic and linguistic back-
grounds should be sampled so that the findings of
this study can be generalized to different populations than the six groups currently sampled.

96

Informal Pilot Survey to Establish
Sensitivity to Sexism in Language

In May 1976, while in the first stages of plannig this research study, an informal survey of elementary school teachers and students was conducted by asking, "Are you (or your students) aware of any problems in choosing between 'he' and 'she' when talking or writing about people in general?" Sixteen out of the seventeen Cleveland area teachers surveyed (third to fifth grade) immediately cited complaints by their students that using "he" all the time was "unfair." Student complainants were usually female. Of the twenty-two neighborhood girls surveyed during May 1976 (aged 4 through 12), nineteen complained similarly. Unfortunately, I have no "empirical data" from boys. Spontaneous offerings of other terms by which girls felt slighted, discouraged or offended included "man-made accomplishments, "our fathers brought forth upon this continent," "mankind," and even "sportsmanship." One astute twelve-year old actually mentioned "cave man" as disturbing since she thought most of the skeletons being discovered were female. Her information is quite accurate.

A related anecdote told by a teacher-friend with junior high age students describes the girls' reaction to a sign observed during their class trip on a ferry boat. The sign explained why boats are called "she." Each reason (temperamentalness, ornamentalness, alluringness) made the girls angrier and angrier, until they complained to the captain that the sign should be removed.

Sample Means and Standard Deviations on Non-Nominal Data

		National Organization for Women	Kiwanis	Middle Aged Men	Middle Aged Women	Male Under- graduates	Female Under- graduates
Age (years)	$\overline{X}$	33.58	49.44	59.08	58.52	19.25	20.86
	s.d.	8.06	12.98	6.55	6.08	1.56	5.67
Sex (1 male;	$\overline{X}$	1.05	0.00	2.00	1.00	2.00	1.00
2 female)	s.d.	0.00	0.00	0.00	0.00	0.00	0.00
Education	$\overline{X}$	2.11	2.33	2.66	3.58	3.50	3.22
	s.d.	0.98	1.12	1.35	0.99	0.60	0.63
Religiosity	$\overline{X}$	2.41	3.47	3.16	2.92	3.19	2.77
	s.d.	1.13	0.56	0.84	0.84	0.92	1.09
Social	$\overline{X}$	2.52	2.55	2.83	2.75	2.17	2.44
Mobility	s.d.	0.65	0.69	0.70	0.65	0.74	0.77
Role	$\overline{X}$	18.55	29.75	27.92	26.39	26.39	21.80
Rigidity	s.d.	7.10	7.84	8.03	5.32	7.16	7.08
Female's	$\overline{X}$	1.67	2.28	2.08	2.03	1.53	1.97
Rank	s.d.	0.79	0.74	0.80	0.74	0.65	0.77
Male's	$\overline{X}$	2.36	1.61	1.72	1.86	2.19	2.05
Rank	s.d.	0.68	0.73	0.74	0.83	0.79	0.79
Unspecified's	$\overline{X}$	1.97	2.11	2.19	2.11	2.28	1.97
Rank	s.d.	0.84	0.85	0.86	0.89	0.81	0.91
Male Mascu-	$\overline{X}$	50.53	46.86	49.97	51.36	56.08	51.05
linity BSRI	s.d.	15.79	11.50	11.30	12.21	18.67	17.81
Male Femin-	$\overline{X}$	71.55	77.19	74.36	73.28	68.17	72.94
inity BSRI	s.d.	13.40	9.40	11.92	10.26	14.59	14.32
Female Mascu-	$\overline{X}$	50.22	54.00	53.13	56.58	55.53	56.28
linity BSRI	s.d.	14.93	10.94	10.68	13.49	10.15	17.68
Female Femin-	$\overline{X}$	63.33	72.69	67.92	72.61	58.78	64.14
inity BSRI	s.d.	13.28	13.88	12.33	14.14	12.31	16.10
Unspecified Masculin-	$\overline{X}$	48.53	49.50	51.97	52.89	52.14	55.55
ity	s.d.	15.56	18.02	16.62	18.23	16.89	18.51
Unspecified Feminity BSRI	$\overline{X}$	65.28	70.36	72.55	68.92	66.80	69.61
	s.d.	14.35	14.21	18.11	13.16	15.58	13.88

(Protocol page 1)

APPENDIX C

Actual Experimental Protocol

Instructions:

Your group has been selected to participate in a study about how people make choices among candidates for a position. Your cooperation will be most appreciated.

You have been given a description of the position to be filled three sets of credentials, and an evaluation form for each of three applicants. After you have read about and responded to the candidates and evaluations, please complete the personal data section but do not state your name anywhere.

Feel free to ask any questions. Thank you.

99

You have been asked to help select a delegate
to the First International World Youth Conference.
Selection from among outstanding high school students has already been done by distinguished teachers,
councilmen, and clergymen, narrowing the field to
three candidates. Your final selection should be
made on the basis of four qualities that join to
form a whole person:

1. Concern for mankind --

   The applicant should view his life as
   an opportunity for serving his fellow
   man beyond his own personal interests.

2. Intellectual excellence --

   The applicant's grade point average
   should reflect his ability to apply
   himself and to achieve highly. The
   range or subjects of interest to him
   should be broad and flexible.

3. Social disposition and patriotism --

   The applicant should show evidence
   of working well with others, such as
   sportsmanship, chairmanship of clubs
   and committees, or person-oriented
   hobbies, and be active in civic,
   democratic, American pastimes.

4. Concern for broad ethical or religious
   values and social responsibility --

   Note that these qualities may take any
   of several forms, depending on the
   background of the individual applicant
   and the particular stage of his life
   which he has reached at the time of
   application. He may or may not be a
   participating member of a religious

denomination; he will often be wrestling with the problems of the relationship between his concerns and the ideas
generated by serious scholarship; he
may have found the institutionalized
form of religion unsatisfactory and
may be in rebellion against it, or he
may have found strength through active
participation in his church or synagogue.

Finally, and above all, the delegate should be
someone you would be proud to have represent America
and to promote the brotherhood of man. Please read
the candidates' qualifications carefully and score
them quickly, as first impressions are most reliable.

CANDIDATE FOR WORLD YOUTH CONFERENCE   27142

Basic Information -- 18 years old, good health and appearance.

High School -- Diploma received June 1975
Ranked fifth in class of 725
Grade point average = 3.80

Honors -- Delegate to regional Student Council conference, 1973
First place, short story contest, 1974
Outstanding achievement in Chemistry and Biology

Activities -- Student Council officer 1972 - 1975
Treasurer, Vice President
Host to Field Service Exchange student from Spain
Horseback riding club
Science tutor
Tennis team
Swim team, senior life saving

Hobbies -- Bicycling, jogging and scuba diving — collecting shells and sea relics,
arranging displays and explanations of sea life for area schools,
libraries, and clubs.
Boating, waterskiing and going to parties are favorite pasttimes.

Statement of Ethical Values: "If I were chosen as delegate to the World Youth Conference, my
most important goal would be to clear up the misunderstandings that the
world has about the U.S.A. As a representative of all Americans, I would
display an interest in world peace, the quality of life, and non-materialistic,
spiritual feelings of goodwill."

102

· EVALUATION   Please guess the degree to which these qualities are either like or unlike the candidate, and circle the appropriate number. Number 1 means very much like the candidate, and 7 means very much unlike the candidate.

	Quality	very like		(Circle)			very unlike			Quality	very like		(Circle)			very unlike
1.	Self-reliant	1	2	3	4	5	6	7	31.	Makes decisions easily	1	2	3	4	5	6	7
2.	Yielding	1	2	3	4	5	6	7	32.	Compassionate	1	2	3	4	5	6	7
3.	Helpful	1	2	3	4	5	6	7	33.	Sincere	1	2	3	4	5	6	7
4.	Defends own beliefs	1	2	3	4	5	6	7	34.	Self sufficient	1	2	3	4	5	6	7
5.	Cheerful	1	2	3	4	5	6	7	35.	Eager to soothe hurt feelings	1	2	3	4	5	6	7
6.	Moody	1	2	3	4	5	6	7									
7.	Independent	1	2	3	4	5	6	7	36.	Conceited	1	2	3	4	5	6	7
8.	Shy	1	2	3	4	5	6	7	37.	Dominant	1	2	3	4	5	6	7
9.	Conscientious	1	2	3	4	5	6	7	38.	Soft spoken	1	2	3	4	5	6	7
10.	Athletic	1	2	3	4	5	6	7	39.	Likable	1	2	3	4	5	6	7
11.	Affectionate	1	2	3	4	5	6	7	40.	Masculine	1	2	3	4	5	6	7
12.	Theatrical	1	2	3	4	5	6	7	41.	Warm	1	2	3	4	5	6	7
13.	Assertive	1	2	3	4	5	6	7	42.	Solemn	1	2	3	4	5	6	7
14.	Flatterable	1	2	3	4	5	6	7	43.	Willing to take a stand	1	2	3	4	5	6	7
15.	Happy	1	2	3	4	5	6	7	44.	Tender	1	2	3	4	5	6	7
16.	Strong personality	1	2	3	4	5	6	7	45.	Friendly	1	2	3	4	5	6	7
17.	Loyal	1	2	3	4	5	6	7	46.	Aggressive	1	2	3	4	5	6	7
18.	Unpredictable	1	2	3	4	5	6	7	47.	Gullible	1	2	3	4	5	6	7
19.	Forceful	1	2	3	4	5	6	7	48.	Inefficient	1	2	3	4	5	6	7
20.	Feminine	1	2	3	4	5	6	7	49.	Acts as a leader	1	2	3	4	5	6	7
21.	Reliable	1	2	3	4	5	6	7	50.	Childlike	1	2	3	4	5	6	7
22.	Analytical	1	2	3	4	5	6	7	51.	Adaptable	1	2	3	4	5	6	7
23.	Sympathetic	1	2	3	4	5	6	7	52.	Individualistic	1	2	3	4	5	6	7
24.	Jealous	1	2	3	4	5	6	7	53.	Does not use harsh language	1	2	3	4	5	6	7
25.	Has leadership abilities	1	2	3	4	5	6	7	54.	Unsystematic	1	2	3	4	5	6	7
26.	Sensitive to the needs of others	1	2	3	4	5	6	7	55.	Competitive	1	2	3	4	5	6	7
									56.	Loves children	1	2	3	4	5	6	7
27.	Truthful	1	2	3	4	5	6	7	57.	Tactful	1	2	3	4	5	6	7
28.	Willing to take risks	1	2	3	4	5	6	7	58.	Ambitious	1	2	3	4	5	6	7
29.	Understanding	1	2	3	4	5	6	7	59.	Gentle	1	2	3	4	5	6	7
30.	Secretive	1	2	3	4	5	6	7	60.	Conventional	1	2	3	4	5	6	7

103

(Protocol page 4)

CANDIDATE FOR WORLD YOUTH CONFERENCE   24967

Basic Information ---   18 years old, male, good health and appearance.

High School   –   Diploma awarded June 1975
Fourth in class of 628
Grade point average = 3.87

Honors   –   Chamber of Commerce Citizenship Award 1972
National Merit Finalist
Award for excellence in English

Activities   –   Community Involvement Council 1971 - 1975
Delegate 1974, National Conference of Christians and Jews
Drama Club
Radio broadcasting club
All-state orchestra, flute, clarinet, piccolo
Red Cross Volunteer, blood bank

Hobbies   –   Creative writing, reading and listening to music of all types. Composing
songs and lyrics, playing in small band at parties and get-togethers.
Going to the beach, hiking, and camping. Am taking up guitar.

Statement of Ethical Values: "If I were chosen as delegate to the World Youth Conference, I
would use the opportunity to show all the other delegates how similar
the peoples of the world really are. I would try to form lifelong friend-
ships and meaningful understandings so that other delegates would
bring back with them warm impressions of our country and its people."

104

Please rate the degree to which these qualities are either like or unlike the candidate, and circle the appropriate number. A number 1 means very much like the candidate, and 7 means very much unlike the candidate.

Quality	very like		(Circle)			very unlike		Quality	very like		(Circle)			very unlike
1. Self reliant	1	2	3	4	5	6	7	31. Makes decisions easily	1	2	3	4	5	6	7
2. Yielding	1	2	3	4	5	6	7	32. Compassionate	1	2	3	4	5	6	7
3. Helpful	1	2	3	4	5	6	7	33. Sincere	1	2	3	4	5	6	7
4. Defends own beliefs	1	2	3	4	5	6	7	34. Self sufficient	1	2	3	4	5	6	7
5. Cheerful	1	2	3	4	5	6	7	35. Eager to soothe hurt feelings	1	2	3	4	5	6	7
6. Moody	1	2	3	4	5	6	7								
7. Independent	1	2	3	4	5	6	7	36. Conceited	1	2	3	4	5	6	7
8. Shy	1	2	3	4	5	6	7	37. Dominant	1	2	3	4	5	6	7
9. Conscientious	1	2	3	4	5	6	7	38. Soft spoken	1	2	3	4	5	6	7
10. Athletic	1	2	3	4	5	6	7	39. Likable	1	2	3	4	5	6	7
11. Affectionate	1	2	3	4	5	6	7	40. Masculine	1	2	3	4	5	6	7
12. Theatrical	1	2	3	4	5	6	7	41. Warm	1	2	3	4	5	6	7
13. Assertive	1	2	3	4	5	6	7	42. Solemn	1	2	3	4	5	6	7
14. Flatterable	1	2	3	4	5	6	7	43. Willing to take a stand	1	2	3	4	5	6	7
15. Happy	1	2	3	4	5	6	7	44. Tender	1	2	3	4	5	6	7
16. Strong personality	1	2	3	4	5	6	7	45. Friendly	1	2	3	4	5	6	7
17. Loyal	1	2	3	4	5	6	7	46. Aggressive	1	2	3	4	5	6	7
18. Unpredictable	1	2	3	4	5	6	7	47. Gullible	1	2	3	4	5	6	7
19. Forceful	1	2	3	4	5	6	7	48. Inefficient	1	2	3	4	5	6	7
20. Feminine	1	2	3	4	5	6	7	49. Acts as a leader	1	2	3	4	5	6	7
21. Reliable	1	2	3	4	5	6	7	50. Childlike	1	2	3	4	5	6	7
22. Analytical	1	2	3	4	5	6	7	51. Adaptable	1	2	3	4	5	6	7
23. Sympathetic	1	2	3	4	5	6	7	52. Individualistic	1	2	3	4	5	6	7
24. Jealous	1	2	3	4	5	6	7	53. Does not use harsh language	1	2	3	4	5	6	7
25. Has leadership abilities	1	2	3	4	5	6	7	54. Unsystematic	1	2	3	4	5	6	7
26. Sensitive to the needs of others	1	2	3	4	5	6	7	55. Competitive	1	2	3	4	5	6	7
								56. Loves children	1	2	3	4	5	6	7
27. Truthful	1	2	3	4	5	6	7	57. Tactful	1	2	3	4	5	6	7
28. Willing to take risks	1	2	3	4	5	6	7	58. Ambitious	1	2	3	4	5	6	7
29. Understanding	1	2	3	4	5	6	7	59. Gentle	1	2	3	4	5	6	7
30. Secretive	1	2	3	4	5	6	7	60. Conventional	1	2	3	4	5	6	7

105

CANDIDATE FOR WORLD YOUTH CONFERENCE   20615

Basic Information --	18 years old, female, good health and appearance.
High School --	Graduated June 1975 Ranked second in a class of 214 Grade point average = 3.91
Honors --	Golden key award for literature, 1974 Citizenship award Award for excellence in Biology Award for excellence in History Finalist, Voice of Democracy
Activities --	Children's guide at Public Library Volunteer Corps; service to elderly Safety Aide, Department of Recreation Folk music club Gymnastics team Scouting, 5 years
Hobbies --	Collecting and designing games from all over the world; puzzles, board games, cards; conducting neighborhood workshops to teach my games to others. Reading, letter-writing, and cross-country skiing are always inviting

Statement of Ethical Values: "If I were chosen as delegate to the World Youth Conference, above all I would try to learn all I could about the other countries represented at the conference. I would prepare myself by reading ahead of time so I would not be full of misimpressions about their cultures, technology, and religions. Though I am very involved in religion, I would be tolerant of and interested in the other belief systems in the world. I wish to share my optimistic attitude about the future of the world with all people."

EVALUATION: Please guess the degree to which these qualities are either like or unlike the candidate, and circle the appropriate number. Number 1 means very much like the candidate, and 7 means very much unlike the candidate.

Quality	very like		(Circle)				very unlike		Quality	very like		(Circle)				very unlike
1. Self-reliant	1	2	3	4	5	6	7		31. Makes decisions easily	1	2	3	4	5	6	7
2. Yielding	1	2	3	4	5	6	7		32. Compassionate	1	2	3	4	5	6	7
3. Helpful	1	2	3	4	5	6	7		33. Sincere	1	2	3	4	5	6	7
4. Defends own beliefs	1	2	3	4	5	6	7		34. Self sufficient	1	2	3	4	5	6	7
5. Cheerful	1	2	3	4	5	6	7		35. Eager to soothe hurt	1	2	3	4	5	.6	7
6. Moody	1	2	3	4·	5	6	7		feelings							
7. Independent	1	2	3	4	5	6	7		36. Conceited	1	2	3	4	5	6	7
8. Shy	1	2	3	4	5	6	7		37. Dominant	1	2	3	4	5	6	7
9. Conscientious	1	2	3	4	5	6	7		38. Soft spoken	1	2	3	4	5	6	7
10. Athletic	1	2	3	4	5	6	7		39. Likable	1	2	3	4	5	6	7
11. Affectionate	1	2	3	4	5	6	7		40. Masculine	1	2	3	4	5	6	7
12. Theatrical	1	2	3	4	5	6	7		41. Warm	1	2	3	4	5	6	7
13. Assertive	1	2	3	4	5	6·	7		42. Solemn	1	2	3	4	5	6	7
14. Flatterable	1	2	3	4	5	6	7		43. Willing to take a stand	1	2	3	4	5	6	7
15. Happy	1~	2	3	4	5	6	7		44. Tender	1	2	3	4	5	6	7
16. Strong personality	1	2	3	4	5	6	7		45. Friendly	1	2	3	4	5	6	7
17. Loyal	1	2	3	4	5	6	7		46. Aggressive	1	2	3	4	5	6	7
18. Unpredictable	1	2	3	4	5	6	7		47. Gullible	1	2	3	4	5	6	7
19. Forceful	1	2	3	4	5	6	7		48. Inefficient	1	2	3	4	5	6	7
20. Feminine	1	2	3	4	5	6	7		49. Acts as a leader	1	2	3	4	5	6	7
21. Reliable	1	2	3	4	5	6	7		50. Childlike	1	2	3	4	5	6	7
22. Analytical	1	2	3	4	5	6	7		51. Adaptable	1	2	3	4	5	6	7
23. Sympathetic	1	2	3	4	5	6	7		52. Individualistic	1	2	3	4	5	6	7
24. Jealous	1	2	3	4	5	6	7		53. Does not use harsh language	1	2	3	4	5	6	7
25. Has leadership abilities	1	2	3	4	5	6	7		54. Unsystematic	1	2	3	4	5	6	7
26. Sensitive to the needs of others	1	2	3	4	5	6	7		55. Competitive	1	2	3	4	5	6	7
									56. Loves children	1	2	3	4	5	6	7
27. Truthful	1	2	3	4	5	6	7		57. Tactful	1	2	3	4	5	6	7
28. Willing to take risks	1	2	3	4	5	6	7		58. Ambitious	1	2	3	4	5	6	7
29. Understanding	1	2	3	4	5	6	7		59. Gentle	1	2	3	4	5	6	7
30. Secretive	1	2	3	4	5	6	7		60. Conventional	1	2	3	4	5	6	7

107

Now that you have studied and evaluated all three candidates, please place the number of each candidate on one appropriate space below:

1 _____ 2 _____ 3 _____
   1st choice   2nd choice   3rd choice

Please state the main reason for your preference.

What do you think the objective of this study was?

     Thank you for your help.

     This final section asks for personal information, however, this is just for interpretation of this study. You will remain completely anonymous, since your name should appear nowhere on these pages. Remember, there are no right or wrong answers to the items that ask for opinions.

1. What is your age? _____

2. Your sex: Male _____ Female _____

3. What is the highest level of education you have completed? _____

4. What career are you in, or if still in school, do you plan to be in?_____

5. What is your religion? (circle)

    Catholic   Other_____
    Jewish   None
    Protestant

6. How religious would you say you are? (circle)

    1. Not at all   2. Slightly   3. Somehwat
    4. Quite   5. Extremely

7. What social class would you say your family belongs to? (circle)

    1. Poverty class   5. Middle class
    2. Lower class   6. Upper middle class
    3. Working class   7. Upper class
    4. Lower middle class

8. Do you expect your eventual social class to be (circle)

    1. Much higher than it   4. Slightly lower
       is now   than it is now
    2. Slightly higher than   5. Much lower than
       it is now   it is now
    3. The same as it is now

OPINION ITEMS:

    1 = strongly disagree   4 = somewhat agree
    2 = somewhat disagree   5 = strongle agree
    3 = neither agree nor
                                    (circle)
1. Women should stay out of politics.   1/2/3/4/5/___

2. People can't be trusted   1/2/3/4/5/___

3. The husband ought to have the say
    in family matters.   1/2/3/4/5/

4. If a child is unusual in any way,
    the parents should try to make the
    child more like other children.   1/2/3/4/5/

5. It is unnatural to place women in
    positions of authority over men.   1/2/3/4/5/

6. Women need to worry about their
    appearance more than do men.   1/2/3/4/5/

7. A wife cannot give as much to her
    career as a husband because she
    is usually more involved in family
    affairs than he is.   1/2/3/4/5/

8. Male teenagers should not be ex-
    pected to baby-sit.   1/2/3/4/5/

9. If a child is allowed to talk
    back to the parents, there will
    be less respect in the family.   1/2/3/4/5/

10. A wife's work should not inter-
    fere with her husband's career.   1/2/3/4/5/

    This concludes the study. If you have any ques-
tions, feel free to ask. Thank you very much for
your help.

REFERENCES

REFERENCES

Agar, M.   "Talking about Doing: Lexicon and Event".
Language and Society, 1974, 3, 14, 83-89.

Albert, E. M.   "Cultural Patterning of Speech Behavior in
Burundi", in Gumperz and Hymes, Directions in Sociolinguistics,
New York: Holt, Rinehart and Winston, 1972, 72-105.

Alker, T.   "The Relationship Between Role Orientation
and Achievement Motivation in College Women". Journal of Personality, 1973, 49, 9-31.

American Psychological Association Task Force on Issues of Sexual
Bias in Graduate Education. "Guidelines for Nonsexist Use of
Language". American Psychologist, 1975, 30, 6, 682-684.

Angrist, S. S.   "The Study of Sex Roles", Journal of Social
Issues, 1969, 25, 1, 215-232.

Bellugi, U.   The Acquisition of Language. Lafayette:
Child Development Publications, Purdue University, 1964.

Bem, S. L.   "The Measurement of Psychological Androgeny",
Journal of Consulting and Clinical Psychology, 1974, 42,
2, 155-162.

Bossard, J. H. S.   "Family Modes of Expression", American Sociological Review, 1974, 10, 2, 230.

Brameld, T.   The Remaking of a Culture: Life and Education
in Puerto Rico, New York: Harper & Bros., 1959.

Brown, R. W.   Words and Things, New York: Free Press, 1958.
Social Psychology, New York: Free Press, 1965.

Brown, R. W. and Gilman, A. 1960, "The Pronouns of Power and
Solidarity" in Seboek, T. (ed.), Style in Language, Cambridge,
Massachusetts: M.I.T. Press, 1972, 253-276.

Brown, R. W.   Psycholinguistics, New York: Free Press, 1970.

Bruce, D.   "Effects of Context upon the Intelligibility
of Heard Speech" in Cherry, C. (ed.), Information Theory.
London: Butterworths, 1956, 245-252.

Brunswik, E.   Perception and the Representative Design of
    Psychological Experiments, Berkeley: University of California
    Press, 1956.

Callary, R. E.   "Status Perception Through Syntax", Language
    and Speech, 1974, 17, Part 2, 187-192.

Campbell, D. and Stanley J. Experimental and Quasi-Experimental
    Designs for Research. Chicago, Rand McNally and Company, 1963.

Cantrell, D.   "Master vs. Mistress", Delta Kappa Gamma
    Bulletin, XLIII, 1974, 32-35.

Cazden, C., et al.   Functions of Language in the Classroom. New
    York: Teachers College Press, 1972.

Child, I., Potter and Levine "Children's Textbooks and Personality
    Development". Psychological Monographs, 1946, 60, 3, 1-7,
    43-53.

Clifford, M. M. and Looft, W. R. "Academic Employment Interviews:
    Effect of Sex and Race", Educational Researcher, 1971, 23,
    6-8.

Coleman, J. S.   "Methods of Sociology", in Bierstedt, R.
    ___ (ed.), A Design for Sociology: Scope, Objectives and Methods,
    Monograph #9, American Academy of Political and Social Science.
    Philadelphia: American Academy of Political and Social Science,
    1969.

Cook-Gumperz, J.   Social Control and Socialization: A Study
    of Class Differences in the Language of Maternal Control,
    London: Rontledge and Kegal Paul, 1973.

Deutscher, I.   "Notes on Language and Human Conduct", un-
    published manuscript, 1967.

Ellis, L. J. and Beutler, P. M.   "Traditional Sex-Determined Role
    Standards and Sex Stereotypes", Journal of Personality and
    Social Psychology, 1973, 25, 1, 28-34.

Ervin-Tripp, M. S.   "An Analysis of the Interaction Between Lan-
    guage Topic, and Speaker", American Anthropologist, 1964, 66,
    6, II, 86-102.

Farb, P.   Word Play, What Happens When People Talk,
    New York, Knopf, 1974.

Feldman, S. D.   "Impediment or Stimulant? Marital Status and Graduate Education", in Huber, J. (ed.), <u>Changing Women in a Changing Society</u>, Chicago: University of Chicago Press, 1973, 220-232.

Ferguson, C.   "Language Problems of Variation and Repertoire", in <u>Daedalus: Language as a Human Problem</u>, Summer, 1973, 32.

Furley, P.   "Men's and Women's Languages", <u>American Catholic Sociological Review</u>, 1944, <u>5</u>, 218-223.

Giglioli, P. P.   <u>Language and Social Context</u>, Middlesex England: Penguin, 1972.

Ghosh, S.   <u>Man, Language and Society</u>, Mouton, The Hague, Paris, 1972.

Glaser, B. and Strauss, A.   <u>The Discovery of Grounded Theory</u>, Chicago: Aldine Publishing Co., 1967.

Glenn, E. S.   "Semantic Differences in International Communications", <u>Review of General Semantics</u>, Spring, 1954, <u>11</u>, 3, 163-181.

Goldberg, P. A.   "Are Women Prejudiced Against Women?" <u>Transition</u>, 1968, <u>5</u>, 28-30.

Gornick, V.   "Consciousness and Raising", <u>New York Times Magazine</u>, January 10, 1971, 22-23, 77-84.

Halas, C. M.   "Sex-Role Stereotypes", <u>Journal of Psychology</u>, 1974, <u>88</u>, 2, 261-275.

Hillman, J. S.   "An Analysis of Male and Female Roles in Two Periods of Children's Literature", <u>Journal of Educational Research</u>, 1974, <u>68</u>, 2, 84-88.

Hughes, E. and Hughes, H.   <u>Where PeoplesMeet: Racial and Ethnic Frontiers</u>, Glencoe, Illinois: The Free Press, 1952.

Hymes, D.   <u>Foundations in Sociolinguistics, an Ethnographic Approach</u>, Philadelphia: University of Pennsylvania Press, 1974.

Hymes, D.   "Origins of Inequality Among Speakers", <u>Daedalus: Language as a Human Problem</u>, Summer, 1973, 59-85.

Jenkin, N. and Vroegh, K.   "Contemporary Concepts of Masculinity and Femininity", Psychological Reports, 1969, 25, 679-697.

Jennings, F. G.   This Is Reading, New York: Teachers College, Columbia University Press, 1965.

Kagan, J.   "Psychological Significance of Styles of Conceptualization", Monographs of the Society for Research in Child Development, 1963, 28, 2,

Kahn, L. G.   "Sexism in Everyday Speech", Social Work, 1975, 20, 1, 65-67.

Katz, J. J.   Semantic Theory, New York: Harper and Row, 1972.

Kelling, G. W.   Language: Mirror, Tool and Weapon. Chicago: Nelson-Hall, 1975.

Key, M. R.   Male/Female Language, Metuchen, New Jersey: The Scarecrow Press, 1975.

Komarovsky, M.   "Cultural Contradictions and Sex Roles: The Masculine Case" in Huber, J. (ed.), Changing Women in a Changing Society, Chicago: University of Chicago Press, 1973, 111-122.

Kramer, C.   "Women's Speech: Separate but Unequal?" Quarterly Journal of Speech, 1974, 60, 1, 14-24.

Kutner, N. G. and Brogan, D.   "An Investigation of Sex-Related Slang Vocabulary and Sex-Role Orientation Among Male and Female University Students", Journal of Marriage and the Family, August, 1974, 36, 3, 474-484.

Labov, W.   Sociolinguistic Patterns, Philadelphia: University of Pennsylvania Press, 1972.

Labov, W.   "On the Mechanisms of Linguistic Change", in Gumperz, J. (ed.), Directions in Sociolinguistics, New York: Holt, Rinehart and Winston, 1972, 516-538.

Lakoff, R.   Linguistic Change as a Form of Communication, in Silverstein, A. (ed.), Human Communication: Theoretical Explorations, Hillsdale, New Jersey: Lawrence Erlbaum, 1974.

Lakoff, R.   Language and a Woman's Place, New York: Harper and Row (Torchbook paperback), 1975.

115

Lane, R.   "Four-Item F Scale", American Political
     Science Review, 1955, 49, 173-190.

Levinson, H., et al.   "Are Women Still Prejudiced Against Women?"
     A replication and extension of Goldberg's study. Journal of
     Psychology, 1975, 89, 1, 67-71.

Maccoby, E.   Psychology of Sex Differences, Stanford Uni-
     versity Press, 1974.

Mannes, M.   "The Problems of Creative Women" in Farber,
     S. (ed.), The Potential of Woman, New York: McGraw-Hill,
     1963, 116-130.

McClelland, D. D.   The Achieving Society, Princeton, New Jersey:
     Van Nostraud, 1961.

McClelland, D. D.   "Wanted: A New Self-Image for Women", in
     Lifton, R. (ed.), The Woman in America, New York: Houghton
     Mifflin, 1967, 173-192.

McNeill, P.   The Acquisition of Language, New York:
     Harper and Row, 1970.

Mednick, M. and Weissman, H. "The Psychology of Women", selected
     topics. Annual Review of Psychology, 1975, 26, 1-18.

Miller, C. and Swift, K.   "One Small Step for Genkeud", New York
     Times Magazine, April 16, 1972.

Moulton, W. G.   "The Nature of Language", Daedalus: Language
     as a Human Problem, Summer, 1973, 17-35.

Murphy, G.   Personality, New York: Harper Brothers, 1947,

National Institute of Education, "Guidelines for Assessment of Sex
     Bias and Sex Fairness in Career Interest Inventories." Measure-
     ment and Evaluation in Guidance, 1975, 8, 7-11.

O'Donnell, B.   "Language in Catechetics", Religious Educa-
     tion, 1974, 69, 5, 542-557.

Philipsen, G.   "Speaking Like a Man in Teamsterville",
     Quarterly Journal of Speech, 1975, 61, 13-22.

Postal, P.   Aspects of Phonological Theory, New York:
     Harper and Row, 1968.

Prather, J. and Fidell, L.   "Sex Differences in the Context and
     Style of Medical Advertisements", Social Science and Medicine,
     1975, 9, 1, 23-26.

116

Probert, W.   Law, Language and Communication, Springfield, Illinois, Charles C. Thomas, 1972.

Rehfisch, T. M.   "Rigidity Scale . . . " Journal of Consulting Psychology, 1958, 22, 10-15.

Rosenkrantz, P., Bee, H., Vogel, S. and Broverman, I.   "Sex-Role Stereotypes and Self-Concepts in College Students", Journal of Consulting & Clinical Psychology, June 1968, 32, 3, 287-295.

Shuy, R.   "Sex as a Factor in Sociolinguistic Research", Center for Applied Linguistics, Washington, D. C., 1969 (mimeographed).

Simon, R., et al.   "The Woman Ph.D.: A Recent Profile", Social Problems, Fall, 1967, 15, 2, 221-236.

Spence, J. and Helmreich, T.   "Ratings of Self and Peers on Sex Role Attributes and Their Relation to Self-Esteem and Conceptions of Masculinity and Femininity", Journal of Personality and Social Psychology, 1975, 32, 29-39.

Steinman, A. and Fox, D. J.   "Male-Female Perceptions of the Female Role in the United States", Journal of Psychology, 1966, 64, 265-276.

Strahan, R. F.   "Remarks on Bem's Measurement of Psychological Androgeny", Journal of Consulting and Clinical Psychology, 1975, 43, 4, 568-571.

Turner, S. A.   "Male and Female Attitudes Toward Sex-Role Concepts in Psychology", 1975, 12, 1, 27-29.

Vygotsky, L. S.   Thought and Language. Cambridge, Massachusetts: The M.I.T. Press, 1962.

Weston, P. J. and Mednick, M.   "Race, Social Class and the Motive to Avoid Success in Women", Journal of Cross-Cultural Psychology, 1970, 1, 284-291.

Whorf, B. J.   Collected Papers on Metalinguistics, Washington, D. C.: U.S. Department of State Foreign Service Institute, 1952.

Williams, F.   "Some Research Notes on Dialect Attitudes and Stereotypes", in Shuy, R. W. and Fasold, Languages and Attitudes: Current Trends and Prospects, Washington, D. C.: Georgetown University Press, 1973.

Williams, J.   "Sexual Role Identification and Personality
    Functioning in Girls: A Theory Revisited", *Journal of Per-*
    sonality, 1973, 41, 1-8.

Witkin, H. A., et al. *Psychological Differentiation*, New York:
    Wiley, 1962.

Wortzel, L. and Frisbie, J.   "Women's Role Portrayal Preferences
    in Advertisements: An Empirical Study", *Journal of Marketing*,
    1974, 38, 41-46.

Wrightsman, L.   "Measurement of Philosophies of Human Nature",
    Psychological Reports, 1964, 14, 743-751.

Yerby, J.   "The Development of an Instrument for Measur-
    ing Sex-Role Orientation in Family Communication Research",
    Unpublished paper presented at Speech Communications Associa-
    tion National Convention, Chicago, December, 1974.

Zimet, S. G.   *What Children Read in School*, New York:
    Grune and Stratton, 1972.